Constance Pessels

The present and past periphrastic tenses in Anglo-Saxon

Constance Pessels

The present and past periphrastic tenses in Anglo-Saxon

ISBN/EAN: 9783337103217

Printed in Europe, USA, Canada, Australia, Japan

Cover: Foto ©Suzi / pixelio.de

More available books at **www.hansebooks.com**

CONTENTS.

Page.

INTRODUCTION 1

The Periphrases in Modern English 1. In Anglo-Saxon:
Resumé of the Views of Previous Investigators 1. Bibliography 6.

I. STATISTICS OF THE PERIPHRASES IN ANGLO-SAXON   11

1. In the Glosses 11.
Vocabularies 11. Lindisfarne and Rushworth Glosses 11.
Benet 15. Vespasian Psalter and Hymns 15.

2. In the Translations 17.
Bede 17. Boethius 25. Gregory 26. Orosius 29. Psalms
34. Benedict 35. Aelfric's Heptateuch 36. Aelfric's Colloquium 37. Aelfric's Interrogationes Sigewulfi 37. The
Gospels 38.

3. In the Original Works 40.
Chronicles 40. Laws 41. Blickling Homilies 41. Aelfric's
Homilies 43. Aelfric's Lives of Saints 46. Aelfric's De
Vetere et Novo Testamento 47. Aelfric's Bede's De Tem-
poribus 48. Basil's Hexameron 48. Wulfstan's Homilies
48. Salomon and Saturnus 49. Poems 49. Tables 51.

II. USES OF THE PERIPHRASES IN ANGLO-SAXON .   . 54
(1) In the Glosses 54. (2) Translations 58. (3) Original
Works 67.

III. THE PERIPHRASTIC TENSES IN OTHER LANGUAGES   75

IV. RESULTS   81

INTRODUCTION.

The periphrasis formed by means of the verb *be* and the present participle, has in Modern English a well recognized meaning. Maetzner [1] (I. 51) says:

"Modern English in this periphrasis makes chiefly prominent the meaning of *continuance,* or *the being engaged in an activity at the time*, and determinations of time often serve to support this meaning".

Koch (§ 88) in treating the present participle dwells on the duration expressed by this tense:

"Es ist Prädicat und wird in den adjectivischen Formen auf das Subject durch das Verb. subst. bezogen .... Das N. E. verwendet es, um die Dauer der Zeitformen gegenüber hervorzuheben: He lives = he is living."

The uses of the periphrasis in Anglo-Saxon have received but hasty treatment at the hands of scholars, though its frequent occurrence in the earliest period of our language caused it to be noticed as early as the time of Hickes. In the "Institutiones Grammaticae" published at Oxford in 1689, he said (p. 53):

"Ab hoc etiam Participio [Praesentis] et verbo Substantivo *Eom*, formatur tempora verborum praesertim verborum *motûs*: ut, he wæs fyligende, *secutus est*. þeos

---

[1] The works are cited by authors. For list see Bibliography, pp. 6 ff.

Pessels.   1

sweoster þa hit dagian ongan wæs utgongende of hire
cleofan, *haec soror, incipiente crepusculo, egressa est de
cubiculo suo.* > þæs ealles nowiht him sylfum wæs gehealdonde, *nihil horum omnium sibi reservavit.* cwæþ he þat
his sawul mid mycele beorhtnysse wære utgongende of
lichoman, *dixit, quod anima ejus cum magno splendore
esset egressura de corpore.*"

In the "Thesaurus", published in 1705, he repeated the
foregoing with these additional remarks (p. 45):

"Saepissime occurrit periphrasticum hoc praeteritum
in versione Boethianâ: ut, ða þ mod þa þillic wæs cweþende
.... Maxime autem omnium Cimbricum hoc praeteritum
affectat ille Pseudo-Nicodemus, in evangelio suo fictitio,
quod publici juris fecit, pro suo in *Saxonicas* literas amore,
Edw. Thwaites."

E. Lye, in his "Grammatica Anglo-Saxonica" prefixed
to the "Etymologicum Anglicanum" (1753) of Junius, and
Owen Manning, who completed Lye's "Dictionarium Saxonico
et Gothico-Latinum" (1772), notice the construction briefly.
It will suffice, here, to quote Manning's words. In the last
named work (I. Gram. Cap. VII) he says:

"Ab hoc etiam [participio praesentis], ope auxiliaris
Beon, formatur interdum praesens, nec non *praeteritum*
Indicativi, ut, Ic eom lufiende. *Ego sum amans*, i. e.
Amo. Ðu spræcende eart. *Tu loquens es*, i. e. *Loqueris.*
Ic wæs ongitende. *Eram intelligens*, i. e. *Intellexi.* Þe
wæs fyligende. *Erat sequens*, i. e. *Sequutus est.* We utofgangende wæron. *Nos egredientes eramus*, i. e. *Egrediebamur* vel *egressi sumus.*"

Manning evidently regards the periphrasis as convertable
with the simple tense.

Bosworth published, in 1823, "The Elements of Anglo-
Saxon Grammar". In this work (p. 139) he observes:

"The imperfect partiable in Anglo-Saxon is formed
by substituting ande, ænde, ende, inde, onde, unde, and
ynde for the infinitive termination, and represent an action

as going on, but not ended: as, He wæs hælende ælce
adle, He was healing every disease. Matt. IV. 23."

March is equally unreserved in pronouncing in favor
of the progressive force of the periphrasis in Anglo-Saxon.
He says (§ 411): "In relation of time action is expressed by
A.-Sax. verbs as in its own nature, *indefinite*, *continued*, or
completed." The forms for continued action are thus given:

"Present continued: ic eom nimende.
Future continued: ic beô nimende.
Past continued: ic wæs nimende."

Moreover, he gives (§ 413, 1) as an example of the
present progressive: "þeos eorðe is berende," and (§ 414, 1)
as an example of the imperfect (pretcrit) progressive: "swa
ic ær secgende wæs".

Mr. Sweet, reviewing Prof. March's work in the *Academy*
(II. 27), says:

It is doubtful whether *ic eom nimende* ought to be
compared with the English *I am taking*. It seems to
be merely an occasional and unmeaning extension of the
simple *ic nime*. Compare the following passage from
Thorpe's edition of Elfric's Homilies (I. 505): 'þa sona
on anginne þæs gefohtes wæs se munt Garganus bifigende
mid ormætre cwacunge', and the translation 'wæs imme-
diately trembling'. Here the idea of continuity is entirely
shut out by the word *sona*. Elfric the grammarian did
not attach any very definite sense to these periphrases
with *habban* and *wesan*, else he would hardly have translated amatus sum by the clumsy *ic wæs fulfremedlice
gelufod*. It seems therefore probable that the delicate
tense distinctions of the modern English verb have arisen
by differentiation from these originally unmeaning and
convertable periphrases."[1]

---

[1] The evidence of Aelfric's Grammar can not be regarded as
conclusive on this point. Aelfric's aim was to give the Anglo-Saxon
pupil as perfect a conception of the force of the various Latin tenses
as words could convey, and for this purpose he renders amatus sum

In the Grammatical Indroduction to his Anglo-Saxon Reader (p. XCIV), Mr. Sweet says: "The periphrases with the present participle have no distinctive meaning".

Mątzner (II. 52) observes:

"The Anglo-Saxon, in the translation of the Bible, has often chosen this periphrasis correponding to allied Greek turns: Johannes väs on vêstene *fulligende* and bodigonde dædbote fulviht. Marc. 1. 4 (ἐγένετο ... βαπτιζων ... κηρύσσων). He väs bodigende ... and deofolseocnessa ût-âdrîfende (1. 39). (ἦν κηρύσσων ... καὶτα δαιμόνια ἐκβάλλων) etc., where the English translation has the simple perfect. The endeavor also often appears to give to the action the stamp of a certain perpetuity: Hî ealle þa on þone cyning *væron feohtende* oð þät þŷ hine ofslægene hâfdon (Sax. Chr. 755).... Frequently, however, no such motive is to be discovered."

Koch does not try to formulate any statement of the use of the periphrasis in Anglo-Saxon, but Müller (p. 242) remarks its varied use:

"Das Activ wird im Ags. nicht selten umschrieben durch die Verbindung von *vesan* mit dem Part. Präs. zur Bezeichnung der Dauer der Thätigkeit (he ... mid him sprecende väs. Bed. IV. 24). Oefters wird indessen die Umschreibung auch gebraucht, ohne dass der Begriff einer Dauer hervortritt."

by the "clumsy" *ic wæs fulfremedlice gelufod*, a collocation perhaps unmatched in his other writings. Similarly in modern grammars we find awkward and unidiomatic expressions used to convey to the student the exact force of Latin, as, e. g., in Madvig's Latin Grammar § 141, "*dicturus sum*: I am he that will say." In the Grammar, Aelfric writes "amabo, ic lufige gyt to dæg oððe to merjen" 131, 5, but in the Homilies he expresses the future by means of *beon* and the present participle: as, "Þa synfullan beoð on hellewite á ðrowigende I, 294, 6. "Þa mánfullan beoð æfre cwylmigende on helle susle", II, 608. 11. In the Grammar, the only form he renders by the periphrasis is the similar Latin periphrasis: as, "menducans est, he is etende; legens est, he is rædende", etc.

Further on (p. 249) he adds:

"Es ist schon früher auseinandergestellt, dass das Part. Präs. mit *vesan* zur Umschreibung des Aktivs gebraucht wird, um eine Thätigkeit als dauernd darzustellen".

Flamme (§ 81), speaking of the periphrasis in the Blickling Homilies, remarks:

"Hier ist zu erwähnen die ausserordentlich häufige Umschreibung [1] des Aktivs durch das Participium des Praesens mit einer Form von *beon, wesan* wodurch das Eintreten in die Handlung, das Verharren in derselben, besonders auch die Gleichzeitigkeit betont wird. Die so umschriebenen Transitiva führen ihr Object bei sich."

Einenkel (p. 273) also attributes to the Anglo-Saxon tense its modern meaning:

"Das Part. Praes. als Prädicat in Verbindung mit dem Verbum Substantivum ist ein häufiger Gebrauch sowohl im A. S. als im Afranz. und dient dazu, der in demselben ausgedrückten Handlung die Bedeutung einer fortgesetzten Thätigkeit, eines dauernden Zustandes zu verleihen".

Schrader (§ 105. 2) denies the Anglo-Saxon periphrasis in Aelfric any of the force it has in Modern English. He says:

"Das part. präs. wird häufig mit *bêon, wesan, weorðan* zu der bekannten Umschreibung verwendet, die aber durchaus noch nichts von der besonderen Bedeutung haben, die sie ne. erlangten".

To decide between these conflicting views the whole body of Anglo-Saxon literature should be studied. In the present investigation, the endeavor has been made to record every occurrence of the predicative participle found in the works examined. While some few have doubless escaped record, they would scarcely be sufficient to vitiate the results reached. A list of the works read and consulted follows.

---

[1] See, however, below p. 71.

BIBLIOGRAPHY.

The following texts have been read:

a) Anglo Saxon:

Aelfr. Col.[1] = 'Colloquium Aelfrici' in Wright-Wülker's 'A. S. and O. E. Vocabularies'.

Aelfr. de Temp. = 'Aelfric's Bearbeitung von Beda's De Temporibus', in Wright's 'Popular Treatises on Science'. London, 1841, pp. 1—19.

Aelfr. de v. et n. Test. = Grein, 'Aelfrik de vetere et novo Testamento, Peutateuch, Josua, Buch der Richter u. Hiob'. Cassel 1872.

Aelfr. Hept. = ib.

Aelfr. Hom. = Thorpe, 'The Homilies of the A.S. Church.' 2 vols., London, 1844, 1846.

Aelfr. L. S. = Skeat, 'Aelfric's Lives of Saints'. London 1881.

Aelfr. Sig. = MacLean, 'Aelfric's A. S. Version of Alcuini Interrogationes Sigewulfi', etc. Anglia Bd. 6, 425—73; 7, 1—59.

Basil = Norman, 'The A. S. Version of the Hexameron of St. Basil's Admonitio ad filium spiritualem'. 2 ed. London, 1849.

Bede = Miller, 'The Old English Version of Bede's Ecclesiastical History of the English People'. Pt. I. London, 1890.

---

[1] The works are usually cited according to the abbreviations used by Callaway (The Absolute Participle in Anglo-Saxon).

Benedict = A. Schröer, 'Die ags. Prosabearbeitungen der Benedictinerregel'. Kassel, 1885.

Benet = H. Logeman, 'The Rule of St. Benet, Latin and A. S. Interlinear Version'. London 1888.

Bl. Hom. = Morris, 'The Blickling Homilies of the Tenth Century'. London, 1880.

Boeth = Fox, 'King Alfred's A. S. Version of Boethius de Consolatione Philosophiae'. London, 1864.

Chron. = Earle and Plummer, 'Two of the Saxon Chronicles Parallel'. Oxford, 1892.

Gosp. = Skeat, 'The Gospels in A. S. and Northumbrian Version Synoptically arranged'. Cambridge, 1871—1887.

Greg. = Sweet, 'King Aelfred's W. S. Versian of Gregory's Pastoral Care'. London, 1871.

Laws = Schmid, 'Die Gesetze der Angelsachsen' 2. umgearbeitete Aufl., Leipzig, 1858.

Oros. = Sweet, 'King Alfred's Orosius'. Pt. I: O. E. Text and Lat. Original. London, 1883.

Poems = Grein-Wülker, 'Bibliothek der ags. Poesie'. 2 vols. Kassel, 1881—1888. Leipzig, 1894. Israel Gollancz, 'Cynewulf's Crist'. London, 1892.

Psalms = Thorpe, 'Libri Psalmorum Versio antiqua Latina cum Paraphrasi Anglo-Saxonica'. Oxonii. 1835.

Salm. and Sat. = Kembles 'The Dialogue of Salomon and Saturnus'. London, 1848.

Vocabularies = See 'Aelfr. Col'.

Vesp. = 'Vespasian Psalter and Hymns', in Sweet's 'The Oldest English Texts'. London, 1885

Wulfst. = Napier, 'Wulfstan: Sammlung der ihm zugeschriebenen Homilien'. Berlin, 1883.

b) Latin.

Bede = Giles, 'Venerabilis Bedae Opera quae supersunt Omnia'. Vols. II and III. Londini, 1843.

Benedict = Migne, 'Regula St. Benedicti'. Paris, 1866 (in Patrol. Vol 66).

Bible = Sabatier, 'Bibliorum Sacrorum Latinae Versiones Antiquae, seu. Vetus Italica, . . . quae cum Vulgata Latina et cum Textu Graeco comparantur'. Paris, 1751.

Wordsworth and White, 'Novum Testamentum Domini
Nostri Christi Latinae'. Oxonii. 1889.

Boeth. = Peiper, 'Boetii Philosophiae Consolationis Libri
Quinque'. Leipzig, 1871.

Gregory = Bramley, 'S. Gregory on the Pastoral Charge:
The Benedictine Text, with an Englist Translation' Oxford, 1874.

The following authorities have been consulted in pre-
paring this dissertation:

Alexander, W. J.: Participial Periphrasis in Attic Prose.
Am. J. Phil. IV. 291 f.

Bernhardt, Ernst: Die Gotische Bibel des Vulfila.
Halle, 1884.

Bosworth, J., The Elements of Anglo-Saxon Grammar.
London 1823.

Bouterwek, K. W.: Die Vier Evangelien in Alt-Nord-
humbrischer Sprache. Gütersloh, 1857.

Bright, James W.: An Anglo-Saxon Reader. New-
York, 1891.

Conradi, Bruno: Darstellung der Syntax in Cynewulf's
Gedicht 'Juliana'. Halle, 1886.

Diez. Friederich: Grammatik der Romanischen Sprachen.
5. Aufl. Bonn, 1882.

Douse, T. Le M.: An Introduction to the Gothic of
Ulfilas. London, 1886.

Draeger, A.: Historische Syntax der lateinischen Sprache·
2. Aufl. Leipzig, 1878.

Einenkel, E.: Streifzüge durch die Mittelengl. Syntax.
Münster, 1887.

Erdmann, O.: Grundzüge der deutschen Syntax. I. Abt.
Stuttgart, 1886.

Flamme, J.: Syntax der Blickling Homilies. Bonn, 1885.

Gering, H.: Ueber den syntakt. Gebr. der Participia
im Gotischen. Zsch. f. d. Phil. v. 423 f.

Gesenius: Hebrew Grammar. Boston.

Green, S. G.: Handbook to the Grammar of the Greek
Testament. London.

Grimm, J.: Deutsche Grammatik. Göttingen, 1837.

Hartel, W.: Lucifer von Cagliari u. sein Latin. Wölff-lins Archiv. III. 1 f.

Hertel, B.: Der syntakt. Gebr. des Verbums in dem angelsächs. Gedichte 'Crist'. Leipzig-Reudnitz, 1891.

Hickes: Institutiones Grammaticae. Oxoniae, 1689.

Thesaurus Grammatico-Criticus. Oxoniae, 1705.

Kaulen Fr.: Handbuch zur Vulgata. Mainz, 1870.

Kempf, E.: Darstrellung der Syntax in der sog. cæd-mon'schen Exodus. Halle, 1888.

Koch, C. F.: Die Satzlehre der engl. Sprache. 2. Aufl., Cassel, 1878. Hist. Gram. der engl. Sprache 2. Aufl., Cassel, 1882.

Köhler, K.: Der syntakt. Gebrauch des Inf. u. Particips im 'Beowulf'. Münster, 1886.

Kühner, R.: Ausführliche Gram. der griech. Sprache. 2. Aufl. Hannover, 1869, 1870.

List, W.: Syntakt. Studien über Voiture. Franz. Stud. I, 10 f.

Lye, E.: 'Grammatica Anglo-Saxonica', in Junius's 'Etymologicum Anglicanum'. Londini, 1753.

Maetzner: An English Grammar. 3 vols. London, 1874.

Manning, Owen: 'Grammatica', in Lye's 'Dictionarium Saxonica et Gothico-Latinum'. Londini, 1772.

March, F. A.: A Comparative Grammar of the A. S. Language. New-York, 1870.

Milroy, W. M.: The Participle in the Vulgate New Testament. Baltimore, 1892.

Mueller, Th.: Angelsächsische Grammatik. Göttingen 1883.

Noder, E.: Tempus u. Modus im Beowulf. Anglia X. 542 f.

Paul, H.: Mittelhochd. Grammatik. 3. Aufl. Halle, 1889.

Planer, J.: Ueber den syntakt. Gebr. des Verbums in dem angelsächs. Gedicht vom Phoenix. Leipzig.

Schmidt, A.: Untersuchungen über K. Aelfreds Beda-übersetzung. Berlin, 1889

Schrader B.: Studien zur Aelfred. Syntax. Jena, 1887.

Schürmann. J.: Darstellung der Syntax in Cynewulf's Elene. Paderborn, 1884.

Seyfarth, H.: Der syntakt. Gebr. des Verbums in dem Cædmon beigelegten angelsächs. Gedicht von der Genesis. Leipzig, 1891.

Sweet, H.: An Anglo-Saxon Reader. Oxford, 1881.

Vernalakens, Th.: Deutsche Syntax. I. Th., Wien, 1861.

Whitney, W. D.: Sanskrit Grammer. Leipzig, 1878.

Winer, G. B.: Grammar of New Testament Greek. Edinburgh, 1878.

Zupitza, J.: Aelfrics Grammatik u. Glossar. Berlin, 1880.

I.

STATISTICS OF THE PRESENT AND PAST PERIPHRASTIC TENSES IN ANGLO-SAXON.

I. IN THE GLOSSES.

VOCABULARIES (13).

The periphrastic tense renders a Latin a) *pres. indic.*
dep. (4): sint behat[ende], pollicentur 87. 22, seðende and
cweðende 340. 17, gemunende 382. 22; b) *imp. indic. dep.* (1):
wæran sacende, emulabantur 398. 35; c) *imp. subj.* (1): ða he
ongitende wæs, animaduerteret 342. 19; d) *imp. subj. dep.* (1):
wæs brucende, potiretur 465. 36; e) *imp. subj. pass.* (1):
waran beotende, intentarentur 426. 12; f) *perf. dep.* (1): acen-
nende wæs, enixa est 392. 15; g) *pres. part.* (1): wæs forbugende, cedens 382. 23; h) *fut. part.* (1): we sind anspecende,
dicturi 391. 9; i) *adj.* (2): berende bið, effeta 394. 26, 474. 11.

LINDISFARNE AND RUSHWORTH GLOSSES (317).

The periphrastic tense renders a Latin a) *pres. subj.
dep.* (1): sprecende wæs, loquar J. 16. 25; b) *imp. indic.* (28):
wæs sittende, sedebat Mt. 13. 1, næbband Mt. 13. 5, 5, gongende Mt. 14. 29, ciegendo Mt. 20, 31, clioppende Mt. 21. 9.
brucende Mk. 1. 6, licgende Mk. 2. 4, cymende Mk. 2. 13,

linigiendo Mk. 2. 15, wyrcende Mk. 3. 8, clioppende Mk. 3. 11,
færende Mk. 4. 37, geongende Mk. 5. 42, gongende Mk. 10. 32,
biddende Mk. 14. 35, sittende Mk. 14. 54, gofrægnende Mk.
14. 61, biddende L. 2. 38, geongende L. 5. 15, hliongende
L. 7. 49, sittende J. 4. 6, geongende J. 5. 9, clioppende J. 7. 28,
stondende J. 18. 16, 18, cliopendeł cuoeðendo J. 19. 6; c) *imp.*
indic. dep. (13): sprecende wæs, loquebatur Mt. 13. 34, fylgende Mt. 26. 58, foerende Mk. 1. 5, sprecende Mk. 2. 2, fylgendo Mk. 2. 15, sprecende Mk. 4. 34, biddende Mk. 5. 10,
sprecende Mk. 7. 35, 8. 32, 14. 31, L. 1. 64, 2. 38, fylgende
J. 18. 15; d) *imp. indic. pass.* (1): wæs ferende, efferebatur
L. 7. 12; e) *imp. subj.* (1): wæs færende, transiret Mt. 20. 30;
f) *imp. subj. dep.* (5): biddende weron, deprecarentur Prol. to
Mt. 9. 6, fore-ondetende L. 2. 3, spellende L. 24. 15, sprecende J. 10. 6, gefroefrende J. 11. 19; g) *perf. indic.* (1):
se þe sellende wæs, qui traditit Mt. 26. 25; h) *perf. indic.*
dep. (117): hoehtende sint, persecuti sunt Mt. 5. 12, fylgende
Mt. 8. 1, wundriende Mt. 8. 10, fylgende Mt. 9. 9, sprecende
Mt. 9. 33, 13. 3, 33, 34, gehatend Mt. 14. 7, fylgende Mt.
14. 13, milsande Mt. 14. 14, sprecend Mt. 14. 27, milsande
Mt. 18. 33, fylgende Mt. 19. 2, 28, gedoemendo Mt. 20. 10,
fylgende Mt. 20. 34, færende Mt. 21. 33, wundrigendo Mt.
22. 22, sprecend Mt. 23. 1, gefoerende Mt. 25. 15, wyrcende
Mt. 25. 16, gestrionende Mt. 25. 16, ofergestrionend Mt. 25. 20,
gestrionende Mt. 25. 22, wyrcende Mt. 26. 10, cyssende Mt.
26. 49, ðrowende Mt. 27. 19, untuende Mt. 27. 52, fylgende
Mt. 27. 55, stelende Mt. 28. 13, spreccend Mt. 28. 18, fylgende Mk. 1. 20, wundrande Mk. 1. 27, fylgend Mk. 1. 36,
færende Mk. 2. 13, fylgende Mk. 2. 14, 3. 7, upp-iornende
Mk. 4. 5, 6, stiornend Mk. 4. 39, færende Mk. 5. 13, milsande Mk. 5. 19, 6. 34, sprecende Mk. 6. 50, færende Mk.
6. 54, stiorende Mk. 8. 30, stiorende ł forbeodende Mk. 8. 33,
milsande Mk. 9. 22, gestiorende Mk. 9. 25, clioppende ł
friende Mk. 9. 36, færende Mk. 10. 17, 12. 1, 13. 1, wyrcende Mk. 14. 6, gefeando Mk. 14. 11, cyssende Mk. 14. 44,
45, fylgende Mk. 14. 54, sprecende Mk. 16. 19, Introd. to
L. XCIII, cunnende L. 1. 1, sprecende L. 1. 70, awoende L.
2. 39, sprecende L. 2. 50, færende L. 4. 1, 14, 42, fylgende

L. 5. 28, awoende L. 8. 55, fylgende L. 9. 11, eft-cerrende
L. 10, 17, sprecende L. 11. 14, 12. 4, drowende L. 13. 2,
sprecende L. 14. 22, færende L. 15. 13, cyssende 15. 20, eft-
færende L. 17. 15, fylgendo L. 18. 28, sprecende L. 22. 4,
gefeando L. 22. 5, dafando L. 22. 5, fylgende L. 22. 39,
sprecende L. 23. 20, fylgende L. 23. 49, sprecende L. 24.
6, 25, eft-færende L. 24. 33, sprecende L. 24. 44, eft-færende
L. 24. 52, ondetend J. 1. 20, 20, fylgendo J. 1. 37, sprecende
J. 6. 63, 7. 36, 8. 12, 20, 40, 9. 29, fuilgendo J. 11. 31,
tæherende J. 11. 35, sprecende J. 12. 29, 36, 41, 48, 49,
15. 3, oehtende J. 15. 20, sprecende J. 17. 1, færende J. 18. 1,
sprecende J. 18. 20, 20, 21, ymbuoende J. 20. 14; i) *perf.*
indic. pass. (5): sawende wæs, seminatus est Mt. 13. 19, 20,
22, 23, unrotsande Mt. 14. 9; j) *plup. indic.* (2): wæs saldend,
dederat Mk. 14. 44, cuoedend Mt. 14. 72; k) *plup. indic. pass.*
(1): hlosnende wæs, suspensus erat L. 19. 48; l) *plup. indic.*
dep. (2): fylgendo uoeron, secuti fuerant J. 1. 40, Introd. to
J. iii; m) *plup. subj. dep.* (2): færende woere, egressus esset
L. 8. 27, sprecend J. 15. 22; n) *fut.* (1): gie bidon stondende,
stabitis Mk. 11. 25; o) *fut. pass.* (1): ondfoende bid, adsu-
metur Mt. 24. 40; p) *fut. perf. dep.* (6): eower hehtende
beoþan, persecuti vos fuerint Mt. 5. 11, sprecende Mt. 12. 36,
gestrionend ł boetend Mt. 18, 15, cyssende Mt. 26. 48, onde-
tende L. 12. 8; q) *fut. perf. pass.* (2): bid ondspyrnende,
fuerit scandalizatus Mt. 11. 6, ondspyrendo Mt. 26. 33; r) *plup.*
subj. (4): were wungiende, mansissent Mt. 11. 23, stigende
Mt. 14. 32, færende Mt. 14. 34, 35; s) *periphrastic pres. indic.*
(18): to cymende, venturus est Mt. 3. 11, þrowende Mt. 7. 12,
to cymende 11. 3, 16. 27, 17. 11, drincende Mt. 20. 22, tocymende Mt. 21. 9, geherende Mt. 24. 6, tocymende Mt. 24. 44,
sellende Mt. 26. 21, tocymende L. 7. 19, 20, 21. 36, J. 1. 15,
27, 6. 14, færende J. 7. 25, lærende J. 7. 35. t) *periphrastic*
pres. subj. (5): tocymmende sie, venturus sit Mt. 24. 42,
sprecendo Introd. to L. li, drouendo Introd. to L. lxv, Introd.
to J. xxxviii, forhycgende J. 5. 45; u) *periphrastic imp.* (5):
þ stydd dæm wæs he tocymende, locum quo erat ipse uen-
turus L. 10. 1, færende L. 19. 4, sellende J. 6. 71. suoeltende
J. 11. 51, sellende J. 12. 4; v) *periphrastic imp. subj.* (6):

weron onfengendo essent accepturi Mt. 20. 10, tocymende Mt.
24. 43, doend L. 22. 23, tocymmende J. 6. 15, sellende J.
6. 64, sueltende J. 12. 33; w) *pres. part.* (12): cliopende ł
ceigende sie, vox clamantis sit Prol. to Mt. v, gefrasende
weron, interrogantes Prol. to Mt. LXXII, stigende Mt. 13. 2,
geondsuarende Mt. 27. 25, febrende Mk. 1. 30, herende Mk.
3. 8, færende Mk. 5. 13, smeande ł đencende Introd. to L. L,
bidend L. 2. 25, slægendo L. 23. 48; x) *pres. part., abl. abs.*
(5): forđor he wæs sprecende, athuc eu loquente Mt. 17. 5.
sitteude Mt. 24. 3, spreccende Mt. 26. 47, útgeongende Mt.
26. 71, spreccende J. 8. 30; y) *pres. part. + imperative of
esse* (1): wæs ł beo đu gemod ł þencende, esto consentiens
adversario tuo Mt. 5. 25; z) *pres. part. + pres. indic. of
esse* (1): ne forđon biđon iub spreccendo ah gaas halig, non
enim estis uos loquentes sed spiritus sanctus Mk. 13. 11;
aa) *pres. part. + pres. subj. of esse* (1): sie sido iuero fore-
gegyrdedo > đæccillae bernendo, sint lumbi uestri præcincti
et lucernae ardentes; bb) *pres. part. + imp. indic. of esse*
(42): wæs þa unfeor suner swina from heom monegra etende,
erat autem non longe ab illis grex porcorum multorum pascens
Mt. 8. 30, licende Mt. 9. 36, etende Mt. 24. 38, drincende
Mt. 24. 38, hemende Mt. 24. 38, sellende 24. 38, haldende
Mt. 27. 54, lærende Mk. 1. 22, bodende Mk. 1. 39, sittende
Mk. 2. 6, đencende ł smeagende Mk. 2. 6, fæstendo Mk. 2. 18,
slepende Mk. 4, 38, cliopende Mk. 5. 5, fælletande ł đærscende
Mk. 5. 5, foedende Mk. 5. 11, licende Mk. 5. 40, sprecende
Mk. 9. 4, sleppende Mk. 14. 40, lærend Mk. 14. 49, biddende
L. 1. 10, becnende L. 1. 22, wæccende L. 2. 8, haldendo
L. 2. 8, wundrando L. 2. 33, bodande L. 4. 44, sittendo
L. 5. 17, hlingende L. 5. 29, đerh-wæccende L. 6. 12, færende
L. 9. 53, worþende L. 11. 14, lærend L. 13. 10, 19. 47, 21. 39,
willnande L. 23. 8, lofaudo L. 24. 53, geblodsando L. 24. 53,
doende Introd. to J. x., fulguande J. 1. 28, fulwuande J. 3. 23;
cc) *pres. part. + imp. subj. of esse* (3): miđđy ana woere
gebiddenda, cum solus esset orans Lu. 9. 18, gebiddende L.
11. 1, gelefendo J. 6. 64; dd) *pres. part. + fut. of esse* (6):
đa steorras heofnes biđon of-feallende, stellae caeli erunt decidentes Mk. 13. 25, spreccend Introd. to L. LVI, suigende L.

1. 20, niomende 5. 10, hæbbende L. 19. 17, sittende L. 22. 69;
ee) *perf. part.* (6): milsande wæs, miseratus Mt. 20. 34, forð-
ongeoude Mt. 26. 39, milsande Mk. 18. 27, frægnend Introd.
to L. LXVIII, færende L. 22. 39, eft-færends L. 24. 9; ff) *fut.*
part. (5): weron ðrowende, passuri Mk. Cap. Lect. XXVII,
fylgendo Introd. to L. LX, gedrowende Introd. to L. LXXIIII,
fylgende Pref. to L. XXXVII, færende L. 14. 31, gg) *infin.* (1)
nælleð ge ðonne sie gemende in morne, nolite ergo esse sollicti
in crastinum Mt. 6. 34; hh) *gerund* (1): halig hundum > bergum
ne is sellennde, sanctum canibus porcisque non dandum Prol.
Matt. XXII. ii) *noun* (1) gif ne were ðes yfel wyrcende, si
non esset malefactor J. 18. 30; jj) adj. (5): gif uutedlice
ego ðiu I yfelwyrcende se I bið, si autem oculus tuus nequam
fuerit, Mt. 6. 23, forletendae Mt. 11. 24, yfelwyrcende Mt.
13. 38, wexende Mk. 4. 17, unberend L. 1. 7.

BENET (9).

The periphrastic tense renders a Latin a) *pres. subj.*
dep. (1): þæt we beon dælnimende, per patientiam participemur
6. 13; b) *pres. indic. periphrastic pass.* (2): þincg sind to
smeagenda, [1] qua requirenda sunt, 26. 11, forsceawiende 84. 6;
c) *pres. subj. periphrastic pass.* (1): sin .. to campiende, sunt
militanda 5. 14; d) *pres. part.* + *pres. indic. of esse* (2):
þæt is mynsterlic campiende, hoc est monasteriale militans 9. 15,
mængcende 14. 14, e) *pres. part.* (3): swa hwa swa he bið
(fuerit) sittende gangonde odde standande ahyldum, vel ubique
sedens, ambulans vel stans inclinato 36. 2.

VESPASIAN PSALTER AND HYMNS (95).

The periphrastic tense renders a Latin a) *imp. indic.*
dep. (2): facen alne deg werun smegende, dolos tota die medi-
tabantur 37. 13, spreocende 40. 7; b) *perf. indic. pass.* (2):
all snyttru heora forswelgende wes, omnis sapientia eorum

---

[1] Logeman § 89 says that the final *a* is owing to the lemma
requirenda.

degluttita est 106. 27, 140. 6; c) *perf. indic. dep.* (75): ða
idlan spreocende is anra gehwelc, vana locutus est unus-
quisque 11. 3, 3, 16. 10, ligende 17. 46, spreocende 21. 8,
frofrende 22. 4, ingongende 25. 1, 11, legende 26, 12, gedæh-
tende 30. 14, smegende 35. 5, spreocende 37. 13, 17, 38. 5,
39. 6, 40. 7, wircende 43. 2, wundriende 47, 6, spreocende
49. 1, 57. 4, mildsende 59. 3, spreocende 59. 8, 61. 12,
smegende 63. 7, spreocende 65. 14, wircende 67. 29, oehtende
68. 27, trymmende 70. 21, spreocende 72. 8, 8, wergende
73. 3, wircende 73. 12, smegende 76. 7, 13, spreocende 77. 19,
elniende 77. 58, ahiðende. 79. 14, legende 80, 16, clyppende 84. 11,
froefrende 85. 17, spreocende 88, 20, gefultemiende 88. 44,
smegende 89. 9, wircende 91. 8, mildsiende 102. 13, spreocende 104. 42, dernlicgende 105. 39, onsumiende 105. 40,
waldende 105. 41, onscuniende 106. 18, blissende 106. 30,
spreocende 107. 8, 108. 3, oehtende 108. 17, spreocende 115. 1,
wreocende 117. 10, 11, resende 118 39, froefrende 118. 50,
52, biddende 118. 58, ymbclippende 118. 61, oehtende 118, 86,
scmegende 118. 129, oehtende 118. 161, onscuniende 118. 163,
biddende 141. 2, ohtende 142. 3, smegende 142. 5, spreocende
143. 8, 11, frofrende V. H'. 2. 2. wreocende V. H. 7. 36,
spreocende V. H. 9. 3, 10. 10; d) *plup. subj. dep.* (1): ða
miclan spreocende were, magna locutus fuisset; e) *fut. dep.*
(2): ah > mid tungan min bið smegende rehtwisnisse ðine
alne deg lof ðin, sed et lingua mea meditabitur justitiam tuam
tota die laudem tuam 34. 28, 70. 24; f) *fut. perf. dep.* (4):
gif min ne bioð waldende ðonne unwemme ic biom, si mei
non fuerint dominati tunc inmaculatus ero 18. 14, elnende
36. 1, 7, onscuniende 70. 24; g) *pres. part.* + *esse* (7): ðu
soðlice dryhten ondfenge min earð ... uphebbende heafud
min, tu autem Domine susceptor meus es ... exaltens caput
meum 3. 4, ongeotende 13. 2, soccende 13. 2, ongeotende
52. 3, soccende 52. 3, sargiende 68. 30, stondende 121. 2;
h) *pres. part.* (2): forðon micel ðu earð > donde wundur,
quoniam magnus es tu et faciens mirabilia 85. 10, wreocende
98. 8.

¹ Vespasian Hymn.

BEDE (299)

A. The Periphrastic Present (14).

I. Accompanied by a temporal modifier (5).

1. Expresses the Progressive Present (4).

It renders a. Latin *pres. indic.* (4): se nu gyt lifigende
is 4. 12, qui nunc usque superest 26. 5, lifiende 216. 23
(334. 23).[1] 448. 10 (* 234. 33),[2] sprecende 348. 4 (* 118. 1).

2. Expresses the Future (1).

It renders a Latin *periphrastic pres. indic.* (1): be dære
we nu sindon sprecende 172. 25, de qua sumus dicturi 288. 16.

II. Without a temporal modifier (9).

1. Expresses the progressive Present (3).

It renders a Latin *pres. part.* (3): Ðæs we scondon ar-
fæslice fylgende > rihtwuldriende 310. 30, hos itaque sequentes
nos pie atque orthodoxe * 76. 19, lædende 88. 19 (134. 21).

2. Expresses the Indefinite Present (5).

It renders a Latin a) *pres. indic.* (1): swylce hit is eac
berende on wecga orum aser > isernes 26. 14, quae etiam
venis metallorum . . . gignit 30. 20; b) *pres. part.* (3): se
wer sepe mid his wif bip slæpende 80. 22 vir . . . dormiens
126. 9, ongeotende 84. 28 (130. 24), winnende 88. 11 (134. 15):
c) *adj.* (1) swylce eac deos eorpe is berende missenlicra
fugela > sæwihta 26, 5, sed et avium ferax terra marique
generis diversi 30. 1.

3. Expresses the Future (1).

It renders a Latin *fut. part.* (1): he nu hwonne on dam
ilcan bip on wuldre arisende 94. 11, resurrecturus in gloria
166. 33.

---

[1] The figures in parenthesis refer to the corresponding Latin text.
[2] The asterisk (*) here denotes the third volume of Gile's ed.
of Bede.

B. The Periphrastic Past (257).

Accompanied by a temporal modifier expresses the Progressive Past (31).

It renders a Latin a) *imp. indic. dep.* (1): under him diacondegnunge micelre tide brucende wæs 272. 18, diaconatus officio sub eo non pauco tempore fungebatur * 26. 2; b) *imp subj. dep.* (1): brucende 316. 16 (* 82. 35); c) *perf. dep.* (1): seo magþ ðreo gearfulle in gedwolan wæs lifigende 142. 14, exinde tribus annis provincia in errore versata est 238. 25; d) *perf. subj.* (2): þæt heofon leoht ealle niht wæs ofer gestondonde > scinende 14. 21. ut super reliquias ejus lux cælestis tota nocte steterit 298. 2; e) *pres. part.* (16): symle mid hio mode wæs flegende 116. 31, ad coelestia regna semper . . . pervolans 196. 18, wunigende 150. 26 (258. 18), restende 272. 1 (* 24. 20). awuniende 300. 1 (* 56. 25), drohtiende 364. 15 (* 134. 33), licgende 378. 21 (* 152. 3), weaxende 382. 5 (* 154. 12), gongende, hleapende, herigende 390. 10 (* 164. 22), þeogende 408. 25 (* 188. 3), weaxende 428. 20 (* 206. 15), inngongende 434. 13 * 210. 30), reccende, styrende 458. 10 (* 244. 9) wuniende 478. 19 (* 294. 5); f) *pres. part*, *abl. abs.* (3): Ða he þa gena wæs . . . wunieude 246. 4, quo . . . demorante 386. 4, weaxende 246. 32 (386. 36), wuniende 458. 7 * 244. 6); g) *perf. part.* (6): he langne tide ealle heora mægþe mid gewede wæs geond farende 148. 21, multo tempore totas eorum provincias debacchando pervagatus 256. 11, wunigende 168. 29 (284 13), 286. 31 (* 42. 32), 452. 26, (* 240. 4), þeowiende 454. 20 (* 240. 33), wuniende 454. 30 (* 242. 5), h) *adj.* (1): wæs Justus se biscop ða gen lifigende 116. 26, Justus autem adhuc superstes 196. 9.

II. Without a temporal modifier (226).

1. Expresses the Progressive Past (70).

It renders a Latin a) *imp. indic.* (2): swa he dælneomende wæs 112. 15, cui ille participabat 190. 31, eardigende 434. 9 (* 210. 25), b) *imp. dep.* (10): þæt wif ðe wæs ðrowiende blodes flownysse 78. 11, quae fluxum patiebatur sanguinis 122. 12, sprecende, scofiende 190. 19 (306. 26)

wyrcende 264. 15 (* 16. 33), sceawiende 288. 15 (*
44. 15), bihealdende 290. 15, (* 46. 11), tosprecende 290.
18 (* 46. 14), upeornende 300. 1 (* 56. 25), spreccende
344. 1 (* 114. 1), brucende 378. 18 (* 152. 1); c) *imp.*
subj. (2): wæs ic in ða ærestan tid minre geoguðhadnisse in
his geferscipe drohtigende 398. 26, nam cum primaevo adu-
lescentiae mea tempore in clero illius degerem * 174. 15,
gongeude 434. 22 (* 212 1); d) *imp. subj. dep.* (9): mid
þy seo foresprecene cwen wæs wunigende on ðam ylcan
mynstre 184. 8, cum praefata regina in eodem monasterio
moraretur 300. 10, wunigende 190. 1 (306. 9), brucende 230. 2
(348. 11), wuniende 262. 28 (* 16. 12), bihealdende 288. 14
(* 44. 11), sprecende, glowiende 346. 33 (* 116. 31),
sprecende 402. 14 (* 176. 29), fordgongende 426. 13 (*
204. 10); e) *perf. subj.* (3): heora æfterfyligendas wæron
deofolgylde folgiende 12. 4, ut . . . successores eorum idolo-
latriam resuscitarint 186. 20, bodigende 12. 21 (240. 15),
lædende 16. 16 (380. 12); f) *perf. indic. dep.* (2): he fædera
weg wæs fyligende 152. 3, patrum viam secutus est 258. 26,
brucende 240. 17 (358. 28); g) *perf. subj. dep.* (1): wæs on-
hyrigende 10. 11, sit imitatus 104. 2; h) *imp. subj. periphrastic*
(1) ða hi wæron to heora swasendum gongende 196. 16, cum
forte ingressuri essent ad prandium 312. 32; i) *pres. part.* (34):
se wæs ða reþan ehteres fleonde 34. 15, clericum quendam
persecutores fugientem . . recepit 46. 3, byrnende 38 14
(48. 31), begytende 94. 28 (168. 10), gefultumiende 98. 11
(170. 25), ðeowiende 172 11 (286. 33), fareude 188. 31 (306. 7),
gefyllende 226. 21 (344. 28), fleonde 236. 18 (354. 29), fylgende 246. 8 (386. 7), forhergende, forneomende 282. 26
(* 38. 14), gesittende 296. 7 (* 52. 19), beornende 300. 2
(* 56. 26), þeowiende 302. 21 (* 60. 15), wæcende 302. 27
(* 60. 23), smeagende 310. 24 (* 76. 13), hweorfende
316. 1 (* 82. 9), restende 340. 4 (* 108. 16), sittende
362. 19 (* 134. 6), gangende 362. 20 (* 134. 7), arisende
378. 22 (* 152. 4), ferende 398. 29 (* 174. 17), hreow-
sende 400. 27 (* 176. 12), gebihtende 404. 23 (* 180. 13),
gefultumiende 414. 9 (* 192. 15), astigende, fallende, gewitende 426. 15, 16 (* 204. 12, 13), uppawallende 426. 26

2*

(* 204. 22), blawende 428. 10 (* 206. 7), efstende 428. 20
(* 206. 16), fordgangende 430. 15 (* 208. 6), hweorfende 462. 1 (* 248. 20), donde 480. 29 (* 312. 9);
j) *pres. part.*, *abl. abs.* (1): wæron þær monige bysceopas
sittende 460. 27, considentibus episcopis pluribus * 246. 19;
k) *perf. part.* (5): he wæs se engel manig ðing sprecende to
him 216. 10. plura locutus 334. 13, utgongende 288. 10
(* 44. 7), ferende 300. 26 (* 58. 19), útgongende 362, 18
(* 134. 6), drohtigende 398. 16 (* 174. 5).

2. Expresses the Historical Perfect (142).

It renders a Latin a) *pres. indic. dep.* (1): se ðe hine
gehatende wæs mid us eoe wunian 316, 28, qui se nobiscum ...
manere pollicetur * 84. 12; b) *imp. indic.* (1): ða ðe lifigende wæron 50. 5, hi qui supererant 70. 1; c) *imp. dep.* (7):
ðær ðe Drihten wæs ... to manum spreeende 84. 7, ubi
Dominus ... hominibus loquebatur 130. 2, frignende 114. 18
(194. 1), 134. 8 (230. 1), biddende 242. 27 (382. 17), cyssende 376. 17 (* 150. 3), biddende 380. 9 (* 152. 21),
spræcende 440. 17 (* 216. 32); d) *imp. subj.* (1): ða he
wæeeende wæs 156. 31, cum evigilaret 266. 25, e) *imp. subj.
dep.* (3): seþe ðas ðing to him sprecende wæs 130. 23, qui
hæe sibi loqueretur 226. 27, spreeende 266. 18 (* 18. 55),
424. 16 (* 202. 19); f) *perf. indic.* (2): he ne wæs ondre-
dende ða beotunge ðæs ealdormanes 36. 10, nequaquam minas
principis metuit 46. 30, lifigende 464. 11 (* 250. 24).
g) *perf. subj.* (2): ðæt Laurentius ... Scottas wæs manigende
10. 32 Ut L ... Seotas monuerit 182. 12, hæbbcnde 12. 17.
(228. 25); h) *perf. indic. dep.* (25): hraþe ða gefremednesse
ðære arfestan bene wæs fylgende 32. 8, mox effectum piae
postulationis consecutus est 40. 28, ðrowiende 34. 8 (44. 26),
yrnende 38. 32 (50. 21), ðrowigende 40. 21 (52. 8), 40. 30
(52. 16), fyligende 48. 14 (66. 27), æfterfyligende 50. 9 (70. 4),
hweorfende 54. 7 (74. 22), forsprecende 84. 28 (130. 25),
ofergeotende 114. 2 (194. 5), biddende 154. 2 (262. 30),
ðencende 194. 15 (310. 29), demende 194. 15 (310. 29),
fylgende 286. 9 (* 42. 4), ondettende 292. 26 (* 48. 33),
hweorfende 292. 32 (* 50. 6), gongende 342. 25 (* 112. 28),
cidende 366. 4 (* 136. 31), hweorfeude 390. 21 (* 164. 33),

utgongende 392. 26 (* 168. 4), 394. 3 (* 168. 13), ongeotende 398, 22 (* 174. 11), ferende 406. 13 (* 182. 34),
þrowiende 416. 29 (* 194. 28), wundrigende 432. 29 (* 210.
4), onscuniende 432. 29 (* 210. 14), ondettende 460. 16
(* 246. 9); i) *perf. subj. dep.* (5): Be Diocletianus rice >
ðæt he Cristene men wæs ehtende 6. 16, de imperio D., et
ut Christianos persecutus sit 42. 26, fyligende 8. 7 (68. 3),
hweorfende 8. 26 (86. 5), trymmende 12. 15 (208. 15), ðrowiende 216. 16 (334. 18); j) *perf. indic. pass.* (3): Se wæs
cumende ungewendre tide on herfeste 44. 28, legio ... in
insulam advecta et congressa est cum hostibus 60. 28, lust-
fulliende 86. 30 (132. 31), gefeonde 474. 22 (* 288. 30);
k) *plup. indic.* (1) his gefera wæs fultumiende þæs godcundan
wordes 250. 23, qui cooperator verbi exstiterat 396. 1; l) *plup.*
indic. dep. (1) ðæt we ær ut of gongende wæron 386. 1, si
forte vel ipsam de qua egressi eramus * 160. 7; m) *pres.*
part. (60): Bryttas to Rome fram Ettio ðam Cyninge wæron
him fultumes biddende 8. 3, Britones ... auxilium flagitantes
non impetraverint 66. 3, cumende 10. 5 (100. 1), 12. 29
(254. 17), forlætende 40. 1 (50. 27), ðeoddende 50. 1 (68. 27),
secende 52. 20 (72. 32), biddende 54. 11 (74. 25), rimende
58. 26 (102. 8), singende 58. 26 (102. 8), wundriende 60. 31
(104. 14), biddende 64. 4 (106. 18), cumende 78. 12 (122. 13),
arecende 80. 11 (124. 29), sæcgende 80. 17 (124. 29), sprecende 94. 22 (168. 8), secende 112. 2 (190. 18), oferhleafende
116. 31 (196. 17), ingangende 132. 19 (228. 10), onbærnende
146. 10 (244. 8), neomende 178. 6 (292. 25), ondrædende
214. 4 (332. 5), bindende 234. 29 (354. 3), forhergiende,
forneomende 240. 24 (380. 19), þreagende 240 25 (380. 18),
donde 250. 22 (394. 33), forlætende 272. 20 (* 26. 6), on-
tynende 284, 20 (* 40. 8), geendiende 286. 5 (* 40. 32),
forebeornende 294. 7 (* 50. 16), gehealdende 294. 22 (* 52.
2), gehatende 328. 19 (* 98. 5), getrymende 348. 11
(* 118. 9), forlætende 348. 21 (* 118. 19), sprecende
354. 5 (* 124. 9), befæstende 358. 23 (* 128. 31), lædende
370. 4 (* 142. 8), togangende 372. 20 (* 146. 6), útgongende 372. 23 (* 146. 7), gesettende 378, 3 (* 150. 8),
streccende 380. 8 (* 152. 19), secgende 380. 18 (* 152. 29),

eefengefeonde 390. 13 (* 164. 15), ingongende 392. 30
(* 168. 8), acegende 398. 23 (* 174. 12), bewergonde
398. 28 (* 174. 16), astigende 404. 10 (* 178. 21), secgende 418. 10 (* 196. 5), cegende 422. 10 (* 200. 6),
cerrende 430. 25 (* 208. 16), eldende 430. 33 (* 208. 22),
gongende 436. 3 (* 212. 15), arisende 440. 11 (* 216. 25),
endiende 450. 8 (* 236. 23), cumende 458. 5 (* 244. 5),
ontimbrende 458. 20 (* 244. 19), geseconde 460. 11 (*
246. 3), arisende 462. 10 (* 248. 29), gefultumiende 468. 29
(* 258. 4), upgangende 476. 10 (* 290. 25); n) *pres.
part. abl. abs.* (2): wæs he se cyning swiðe gefeonde in þæs
biscopes cyme 302. 8, imo multum gaudente rege * 60, 3,
blinnende 386. 13 (* 160. 18); o) *perf. part.* (18) ða wæs
gangende sum ðara broþra in to him 186. 24 ingressum ad
eum quidam de fratribus 302. 21, forðgongende 42. 4 (52. 24),
eldende 192. 11 (308. 18), cyþende 228. 20 (346. 29), ge-
treomende 236. 4 (354. 13), onhyrgende 246. 4 (386. 4),
þurhfærende 250. 24 (396. 3), utgongende 284. 10 (* 38. 26),
hweorfende 330. 8 (* 98. 27), inhyrgende 332. 17 (*
102. 7), gongende 352. 16 (* 122. 27), biddende 374. 2
(* 146. 19), gongende 382. 21 (* 154. 29), blissiende
390. 18 (* 164. 32), onhyrgende 396. 10 (* 170. 24),
fylgende 414. 15 (* 192. 20), sittende 460. 13 (* 246. 6),
ingongende 438. 5 (* 214. 20); p) *fut. part.* (2): he ða
wæs smeagende mid ðone apostolicon Papan Bonefactio 108. 8,
cum apostolico Papa B. tractaturus 184. 34, gebiddende 386. 10
(* 160. 17); q) *infin.* (3): he wæs brucende engillicre ge-
syhþe 210. 14, angelice meruit visione perfrui 328. 11, gongende 372. 32 (* 146. 15), sprecende 462. 19 (* 250. 2);
r) *supine* (1): se wæs middangeard forhycgende 412. 17, ipse
contemtu mundi * 190. 28; s) *paraphrase* (4): sona ic wæs
wyrpende 394. 3, statim melius habere incipio * 168. 14,
þehtende 416. 17 (* 194. 16), sprecende 416. 17 (* 194. 16),
wundrigende 432. 29 (* 210. 14).

3. Expresses the Pluperfect (5):

It renders a Latin a) *perf. indic. dep.* (4): be ðam we
foresprecende wæron 6. 61, de quibus praefati sumus 108. 14,
foresprecende 202, 25 (320. 6), sprecende 276. 28 (* 30. 26),

foresprecende 324. 11 (* 90. 19); b) *pres. part.* (1): forlætende 262. 32 (* 16. 16).

4. Expresses the Passive (1).

It renders a Latin *pres. part.* (1): neh ceastra gehwylce > land wæs forhergiende[1] 52. 29, proximas quasque civitates agrosque depopulans 74, 4.

5. Expresses the Future Preterite[2] (8). It renders a Latin a) *periphrastic imp. indic.* (1): on æfenne þære neahte þe he of worulde gongende wæs 346. 29, nocte qua de seculo erat exiturus No. 116. 26; b) *periphrastic imp. subj.* (4): ðis syndon ðan fyr ða ðe middangeard wærun forbærnende > forneomende 212. 25, audivi hos esse ignes, qui mundum succendentes essent consumturi 330. 26, gelædende, onfonde 284. 22 (* 40. 10); c) *fut. part.* (3): he wæs. endebyrdlice settende be muneca life 108. 11, de vitae monachorum et quiete ordinaturus 186, 2, farende 458. 15 (* 244. 15), recende 458. 16 (* 244. 16).

C. The Present Subjunctive (4).

1. Expresses the Indefinite Present (1).

It renders a Latin *infin* (1): þonne hie syn begongende weoroldlicne comphad 480. 11, satagunt . . . . monasterialibus ascribere votis, quam bellicis exercere studiis * 294. 32.

2. Expresses the Future (3):

It renders a Latin a) *periphrastic pres. subj.* (2): oððe hwilcne ende syndrigo þing hæbbende seondon 476. 30, quemve habitura sint finem singula * 292. 14, hæbbende 480. 12 (* 294. 34); b) *pres. part.* (1): ðy læs we ænige tide ussum licumlicum unalefednessum sion þiowiende 356. 12, ne forte nos tempore aliquo carnis illecebris servientes * 126. 17.

---

[1] MS. B. reads *forheregcode.*

[2] "If we regard an occurrence as impending in the past instead of in the present we have the *future preterite* tense (I should see, he would see)". Henry Sweet, *A New English Grammar,* I. § 278.

D. The Past Subjunctive (24).

1. Expresses the Progressive Past (10).

It renders a Latin a) *pres. indic.* (1): cwæð, þæt he
ða gena lifgende wære 378. 12, qui nunc usque superest
* 150. 30; b) *imp. indic. pass.* (1) awritan is, þæt hi wæron
todælende heora weoruld god. 66. 2, dividebatur singulis
prout cuique opus erat 108. 15; c) *imp. subj.* (1): sæde eac þ se
ylca brothur ða gyt on ðam mynstre lifigiende wære 188. 1,.
loquebatur, superesset in eodem monasterio jam juvenis ille
304. 9; d) *imp. subj. dep.* (1): þa frugon heo... mid hwone
heo sprecende wære 290. 27, interrogata, cum quo loqueretur
* 46. 23; e) *perf. indic. pass* (1) seo sona wære to ðon swiðe...
hefigende þæt se earm wæs . . . gecerred 392. 4; gravatum
est * 166. 16; f) *pres. part.* (3): swa swa heo biddende wære
his ondsware 290. 17, quasi responsum ejus . . . expectans
* 46. 14, licgende 392. 7 (* 166. 18), bensiende 402. 10
. (* 176. 25); g) *pres. part., abl. abs.* (1) seo sona wære to ðon
swiðe weaxende, etc. 392. 4, quo mox increscente * 166. 16; h)
infin. (1) ma he wunode þæt he for þam ecan rice symble won
> God biddende[1] wær, 188. 6 pro æterno regno semper
laborare ac deprecari solebat 304. 15.

2. Expresses the Future Preterite (9).

It renders a Latin a) *imp. subj. dep.* (2): ðæt ðæs
wæstmas eard wære uppeornende 366. 30, ut illius frugis ibi
potius seges oriretur * 138. 25, sprecende 416. 18 (* 194. 17);
b) *periphrastie imp. subj.* (5): þæt hi ðonne wæron ðurh heora
handa deaþes wræc ðrowiende 102. 25, per horum manus
ultionem essent mortis passuri 176. 26, ferende 286. 25
(* 42. 22), sweltende 288. 20 (* 44. 17), útgongende 296. 11
(* 52. 23), cummonde 368. 20 (* 140. 18); c) *fut. perf.
dep.* (1): ðonne wif cennede wære 76. 5, cum vero enixa
fuerit mulier 120. 7; d) *pres. part.* (1): þa ongan . . . him
ondrædan, þonne he to deaðe cumende wære 294. 26, timere
coepit homo . . . ne ad martem veniens * 52. 7.

---

[1] So Smith; Miller reads *bletsode*.

3. Expresses the Historical Perfect (5).

It renders a Latin a) *pres. indic.* (1): se þe lifigende
wære ðæs hades hæfde mihte 146. 21 is, qui supcrest, censors
ejusdem gradus habeat 246. 45; b) *pres. part.* (3): secgað
men þæt he eac were mid gehate hine. seolfne bindende
306. 23, voto se obligans * 70. 26, wiðwinnende 368. 16
(* 140. 14), arisende 470. 6 (* 284. 9; c) *infin.* (1): efnblissende
62. 18 (104. 30) [1].

BOETHIUS (20).

A. The Periphrastic Present (14).

I. Accompanied by a temporal modifier expresses the
Progressive Present (6).

It renders a Latin a) *pres. indic.* (1): ðeah biþ simle
corn ðære soþfaestnesse sæd on þare sawle wunigende 156. 3,
haeret profecto semen introrsum 81. 11; b) *pres. subj.* (1):
eala þæt nan wuht nis fæste stondondes weorces a wuniende
on worulde 26. 22, constat . . . ut constet genitum nihil 31;
18; c) *pres. part.* (2): ðonne miht ðu ongitan þæt þa godan
bioþ simle weallende 172. 23, semper quidem potentes bonos
esse 89. 25, waldende 178. 5 (92. 40). *No Latin correspondence* (2): gifende 258. 5, lociende 258. 8.

II. Without a temporal modifier (8).

1. Expresses the Progressive Present (4).

It renders a Latin *pres. indic.* (1): ic eom ealne þone heofon
ymbhweorfende 20. 35, rotam uolubile orbe versamus 27. 28.
Paraphrase (2): libbende 68. 13, farende 152. 4; *no Latin
correspondence* (1): smugende 80. 27.

2. Expresses the Future (1).

It renders a Latin *fut. perf.* (1): ac þonne heo hwam
from hweorfende beoð 18. 16, cum discesserit 25. 39.

---

[1] In the following examples the participle has lost its verbal
force, and has become an adjective: gymende > smeagende 25 (23. 12),
freomigende 14. 20 (296. 1), wæstmberende 98. 12 (170. 24), weallende
154. 22 (264. 3), scinende 210. 4 (328. 1), halwende 214. 23 (332. 24),
sorgende 282. 29 (* 38. 16), weallende 370. 1 (* 142. 4), beofiende 424. 1
(* 202. 2), liciende 436. 25 (* 214. 12).

2. Expresses the Indefinite Present (3).

It renders a Latin *perf. part.* (1): þa . . . bioþ uton ymbstandende mid miclon gewerscipe hiora þegna 186. 4, saeptos tristibus armis 95. 3; *no Latin correspondence* (2): an ðara gecynda is þæt heo biþ wilnigcnde 132. 4, irsiende 132. 4.

B. The Periphrastic Past Indicative (5).

1. Expresses the Progressive Past (4).

It renders a Latin *perf. indic.* (2): ða þæt Mod þa þillic sar cweþende wæs > þis leoþ singende wæs 8. 23, haec ubi continnato dolore delatraui 18. 1; *paraphrase* (2): libbende 58. 17, wariende 76. 7.

2. Expresses the Historical Past (1).

It renders a Latin *pres. indic.* (1): be þam wæs geo singende sum sceoþ 106. 32 unde . . . tragicus exclamat 62. 2.

C. The Periphrastic Past Subjunctive (1).

Expresses the Progressive Past (1).

It renders a Latin *noun* (1): gif þu nu wære wegferende 46. 25, si vitae huius callem uacuus uiator intrasses 39. 97 [1].

GREGORY (30).

A. The Periphrastic Present (13).

I. Accompanied by a temporal modifier (2).

1. Expresses the Progressive Present (1).

It renders a Latin *pres. indic pass.* (1): se symble bið cuyssende ðæt scip 58. 5, in qua semper cogitationum procellis navis cordis quatitur 34. 14.

2. Expresses the Future (1).

It renders a Latin *fut. indic.* (1): se þe ryhtwis bið, he bið a sellende 336. 5, qui justus est, tribuet 260. 15.

---

[1] In the following examples the participle has no verbal force: þurhwuniende 30. 10, hreosende 34. 22, fleonde 144. 36, wealdend 176. 17, sorgiende (text reads forgiende) 196. 7, untyriende 252. 20.

II. Without a temporal modifier (11).

1. Expresses the Indefinite Present (7).

It reuders a Latin a) *pres. indic.* (1): ac his mod bið
swiðe yðegende 168. 11. cor defluit 124. 11; b) *pres. subj.*
dep. (1): hu æghwelc syn bið sætigende dæs ðcondon monnes
160. 24. nam cum unum quodque peccatum quomodo profi-
cientibus insidietur 118. 9; c) *pres. part.* (3): he bið swiðe
hræðe ymbe hiene sprecende 92. 3, de se protinus loquentes
facit 62. 16, gnorniende 224. 10 (170. 8), yðgiende 409. 35
(330. 16); d) *gerund* (2); swa hwa ðonne swæ ða wrohte
bið sawende 358, 25 quisquis seminando jurgia 278. 26,
lærende 170. 13 (126. 9).

2. Expresses tbe Future (4).

It renders a Latin a) *pres. indic.* (1): ðonne betweox
oðrum mægenum bið ðeonde 86. 25, cumque inter virtutes
ceteras . . . proficit 58. 23; b) *pres. indic. periphrastic* (3):
se þe demende is cwicum and deadum 96. 13, qui judicaturus
est vivos et mortuos 66. 17. gewitende 441. 20 (368. 16),
ðurhwuniende 441. 21 (368. 18).

B. The Periphrastic Past (7).

1. Expresses the Progresive Past (2).

It renders a Latin a) *pres. indic.* (1): On ðæs sacerdos
hrægle wæron bellan hangiende 92. 15, vestimentis itaque
illius tintinnabula inhærent 62. 29; b) *pres. part.* (1): Forðæm
ðe he wæs eall biernende 309. 10 totus ardens 238. 7.

2. Expresses the Historical Perfect (5).

It renders a Latin a) *pres. indic. pass.* (1) To swelcum
monnum Salomon wæs sprecende 286. 11, quibus sub audi-
toris . . . apud S. dicitur 216. 24; b) *pres. indic. dep.* (2):
næron ge no min gemunende 150. 21, mei non es recordata
110. 4, ferende 46. 4 (24. 14): c) *pres. part.* (1): Locu nu,
hu Dryten wæs sprecende of hefonum 443. 26, ecce de coelo
Dominus loquens 372. 1. *Paraphrase* (1) biddende 256. 16
(194. 18).

C. The Periphrastic Present Subjunctive (7).

I. Accompanied by a temporal modifier expresses a Progressive Present (2).

It renders a Latin *perf. indic. dep.* (2): butan mon simle swincende and wyrcende sie gōd weorc oð ende 445. 15, operatum est 372. 25.

II. Without a temporal modifier (5).

1. Expresses the Progressive Present (1).

It renders a Latin *pres. part.* (1): gehine lufige swelce he wunigende sie 395. 31, in cassum cor quasi manentea figitis 314. 5.

2. Expresses the Imperative (4).

It rendors a Latin a) *pres. part.* (2) hie sie . . . rædende and wituigende 124. 4 consulens et sæviens 86. 25; b) *gerund* (1): he ne sie gidsiende oðera monna æhta 60. 13, quid ad aliena cupienda non ducitur 36. 10; c) *Noun* (1): ac sie se lareow . . . efneðrowiende on hiera geswincum 96. 22, sit rector singulis compassione proximus 66. 25.

D. The Periphrastic Past Subjunctive (2).

1. Expresses the Progressive Past (1).

It renders a Latin *pres. part.* (1): se wære feohtende wið ðæm willan his modes, 423. 18 video aliam legem . . . repugnantem legi mentis meæ 346. 13.

2. Expresses the Historical Perfect (1).

It renders a Latin *perf. indic. dep.* (1): hit is awritan ðæt Dina wære út gongende 415. 14 Egressa est Dina 336. 12.

E. The Copula *weordan* and the Present Participle (1).

The Periphrastic Present expresses the Future (1).

It renders a Latin *adj.* (1): ðinra synna ne weorðe ic gemunende 413. 23, peccatorum tuorum memor non ero 334. 4. [1]

---

[1] In the following examples the participles are predicative a) adjectives: ðeonde 58. 12 (34. 20), scinende 66. 25 (42. 19), rempende

OROSIUS (235).

A. The Periphrastic Present (13).

I. Accompanied by a temporal modifier expresses the Progressive Present (4).

It renders a Latin *pres. ind.* (1): þe giet ricsiende sindon 58. 30, quod usque ad nunc manet 59. 23. *No Latin correspondence* (3): se ilce þe giet sittende is > wendende 64. 2, ricsiende 62. 30.

II. Without a temporal modifier (9).

1. Expresses the Progressive Present (1). It renders a Latin *pres. indic.* (1): hiere onweald is .. hreosende 76. 2, moles contremiscunt 75. 28.

2. Expresses the Indefinite Present (8). It renders a Latin a) *pres. indic.* (3): seo is irnende of norððæle 8. 15, sub plaga septentrionis Tanaim fluvium fundunt 9. 11, flowende 12. 35 (13. 18), irnende 74. 18 (76. 2); b) *pres part.* (1): seo .. is irnende þurh middewearde Babylonia burg 74. 3, medium B. interfluentem 75. 2; c) *infin.* (1): he is east irnende from eastdæle 12. 26, orientem versus prolabi 13. 22. *No Latin correspondence* (3): irnende 14. 32, biddende 48. 23, giddiende 94. 29.

B. The Periphrastic Past (211).

I. Accompanied by a temporal modifier expresses the Progressive Past (81).

It renders a Latin a) *pres. indic.* (1): God siþþan longsumlice wrecende wæs 58. 17 mundus arguitur 59. 11; b) *pres. indic. pass.* (1): he wæs vi dagas on þa burg feohtende 212. 3, sex continuis diebus pugnatur 213. 7; c) *imp. indic.* (1): he wæs sinþyrstende monnes blodes 130. 31, semper sitiebat

148. 12 (108. 3), wandigende 148. 14 (108. 4), welwillende 234. 17 (178. 8), gewitende 298. 8 (226. 7), 298. 10 (226. 8), deorfende 326. 8, 9 (252. 14), fleonde 332. 14 (258. 1), ðurhwuniende 393. 33 (312. 6), fleondo 427. 22 (352. 8), libbinde 429. 24 (354. 13); b) noun: leogende 150. 21 (110. 3).

cruorem 131. 26; d) *imp. indic. pass.* (2): þe ær wæron LXX
wintra wið Romani winnende 100. 29, qui per septuaginta
annos conficiebantur 10. 123, dreogende 140. 27 (141. 29);
e) *imp. subj.* (2): he wæs þæt folc þonan ut sleande > hienende 168. 29 prosterneret i 69. 21; f) *perf. indic.* (11): he
wæs heriende > feohtende fiftig wintra 28. 28, quinquaginta
annis bellis egit 29. 33, dreogende 30. 16. (31. 10), winnende
40. 32 (41. 16), 42. 31 (43 25), wendende 48. 10 (49. 3),
winnende 56. 10 (57. 7), dreogende 68. 31 (69. 10), æfterfylgende 74. 3 (75. 22), þyrstende 76. 34 (77. 18), winnende
218. 30 (219. 28); g) *perf. indic. pass.* (1): hie dreogende
wæron XIII winter 202. 31. quod gestum est annis septemdecim
203. 16; h) *perf. indic. dep.* (2): þær wæron fiftene gear þæt
lond herigende > westende 44. 19 ubi per XV annos sine
pace immorati 45. 15; i) *plup. indic.* (1): Rædgota dæghwamlice wæs blotende diofolgildum mid monslihtum 296. 13, qui
omnem Romani generis sanguinem diis suis propinare devoverat
297. 9; j) *plup. subj.* (1): mid þæm þe he sprecende wæs to
his geferum 84. 33, cum ... dixisset 85. 24; k) *pres. part.*
(9): hio ðyrstende wæs on symbel mannes blodes 30. 27 sanguinem sitiens 31. 18, brucende 32. 7 (33. 8), winnende 56. 15
(57. 11), sittende 56. 26 (57. 20), hergende 94 1 (95. 1),
94. 2 (95. 1), bærnende 94. 2 (95. 1), winnende 114. 15
(115. 15), biernende 262. 2 (261. 28); l) *pres. part., abl.*
abs. (1): on þære tide wæron Dioclitie III cyningas on winnende
278. 24 Carausio rebellante 279. 19; m) *perf. part., abl. abs.*
(3): Perseus wæs ealne þone gear Romane swiðe swencende
208. 13, profligato multis proelis exercitu Romano 209. 12,
winnende, sleande 46. 5 (45. 26); n) *perf. part.* (1): on ðære
hwile þe he þær winnende wæs 130. 9 illum bello intentum
131. 11; o) *fut. perf. periphrastic* (1): on þære hwile ...
Amicor ... wæs færende 170. 13, transfugiturus fuerit 171. 9;
p) *infin.* (1): þe þæt ilce wæron dreogende cc wintra 214. 4,
cum per annos ducentos hostem nec repellere proterat 215. 11;
q) *substantive* (14): Uesoges ... wæs winnende of suððæle
Asiam, oð 44, 4, miscere bello studens 45. 4, sittende, feohtende 50. 13 (51. 3), winnende 66. 24 (67. 4), drincende 76. 18
(77. 9), feohtende 80. 25 (81. 14), winnende 112. 24 (113. 14),

hiende 120. 11 (121. 8), bærnende, sleando 120. 12 (121. 8),
færende, winnende 130. 20 (131. 18), dreogende 134. 7 (135. 5),
sittende 186. 4 (187. 1). *No Latin correspondence* (28): yrnende 19, 33, piniende 36. 31, winnende 44. 27, wraciende
50. 21, þrowiende 54. 26, dreogende 58. 4, winnende 66. 21,
wuniende 72. 1, farende 76. 28, winnende 88. 22, dreogende
90. 18, æfterfylgende 92, 14, weaxende 104. 18, cyðende 104. 19,
donde 108. 29, winnende, feohtende 114. 6, hergiende 114. 30,
winnende 116, 2, hergende 118. 19. sierwende 118. 19, dreogende 182. 4, sleande 200. 20, wuniende 220. 2, dreogende
224. 28, þafiende 230. 17, æfterfylgende 236. 29, dreogende
238. 3.

II. Without a temporal modifier (130).

Expresses the Progresive Past (25).

It renders a Latin a) *pres. indic.* (1): se cyning . . .
mid oferheortnesse him wæs waniende 166. 10, accussat et
deflet 167. 10; b) *pres. subj.* (1): seðdan ðær wæs standende[1]
wæter ofer þam lande 32. 11, nunc mare superfusum tegat
33. 15; c) *perf. indic.* (2); wæs byrnende fyr up of þære
eorþan 160. 24, extorruit 161. 15, biernende 234. 8 (235. 8);
d) *perf. indic. pass.* (1) ac Romane . . . Gode þowiende
wæron 64. 11, aequitas in rege servata est 65. 6; e) *pres.*
part. (1): he þider mid firde færende wæs 174. 2, iter cum
exercitu faciens 175. 4; f) *infin.* (2): an gylden hring . . .
wæs fram þæm heofone bradiende niþer oþ þa eorðan >
wæs eft farende wið þæs heofones 234. 10, globum coloris
aurei coelo ad terram devolvi, rursus in sublimi ferri 235. 6;
g) *substantive* (2): seo corpe wæs cwaciende > berstende
88. 11, in Italia terrae motus fuerunt 89. 9. *No Latin corre-*
spondence (15): þe Babylonie mid monigfealdum unryhtum . . .
libbende wæran 64. 8, iernende 66. 1, feallende, biddende
66. 2, brociende 70. 11, wuniende 76. 21, þencende 76, 24,
winnende 100. 1, 160. 6, æfterfylgende 168. 32, farende
226. 6, weaxende 232. 26, micliende 252. 12, þencende
292. 24.

---

[1] This may also he construed as an appositive participle.

2) Expresses the Historical Perfect (105).

It renders a Latin a) *pres. indic.* (5): he wæs feohtende
wið Sciððie 30. 12, oppugnat 31. 3, æfterfolgiende 44. 16
(45. 12), ierniende 54. 2 (53. 22), sprecende, geomriende
80. 34 (81. 18); b) *pres. indic. pass.* (2): he him unwinnende
wæs 30. 5, dum vincitur 31. 3, winnende 148. 35 (149. 19);
c) *imp. subj.* (2): dær micelne hungor þoliende wæron 66. 18.
fames domi timerentur 67. 3, forhiende 200. 29 (201. 15);
d) *perf. indic.* (15): his cniht Iustinus wæran ðus singende
32. 29, qui inter caetera sic ait 33. 28, feohtende 30. 19
(31. 12), æfterfylgende 38. 22 (39. 12), farende 44. 6 (45. 5),
donde 50. 3 (49. 17), winnende 56. 8 (57. 4), farende 74. 6
(75. 3), teonde 88. 20 (89. 16), donde 148. 2 (149. 2), 188.
18 (189. 14), biddende 202. 10 (203. 2), irnende 222. 6
(223. 2), farende 236. 9 (237. 5), 236. 20 (237. 20), mænende
242. 19 (243. 7); e) *perf. indic. pass.* (1): ac þa monigfaeldan
iermþo þa werigan burg· swiþe brociende wæron 70. 11,
cessatum tamen a mortibus non est 71. 9; f) *plup. subj.* (3):
manigfeald geligre fremmende wæs 30. 29, concubitu ob-
lectasset 31. 18, fleonde 76. 15 (77. 7), ehtende 134. 14
(135. 9); g) *pres. part.* (8): þa wæron swiðe hreolice berstende
38. 8. vesices effervescentes 39. 4, utsionde 38. 8 (39. 4),
sceorfende 38, 12 (39. 7), biddende 82. 2 (83. 10), lærende
82. 29 (83. 16), cirrende 116. 34 (119. 2), ˉbrædende 166.
19 (167. 9), farende 284. 31 (285. 30); h) *perf. part.* (3):
him Romane þæt swiðe ondreadende wæron 70. 1, quo metu
consternati Romani dictatorem creant 71. 1, cirrende 236.
14 (237. 10), farende 246. 7 (247. 5); i) *perf. part., abl.
abs.* (1): þonon wæs færende on Nilirice 124. 8, translato
abhinc bello 125. 4, j.) *infin.* (4): hie selfe fleonde wæron
82. 26, aperte fugere persuasit 83. 13, fleonde 128. 7 (129. 4),
bradiende 234. 10 (234. 5), farende 234. 11 (235. 5): k) *gerund* (2): þæt folc wæron hergende on Romane 100, 31, bel-
lando et caedendo pervenerant 101. 28, feohtende 172. 22
(173. 18); l) *substantive* (9): se scop wæs secgende 34. 16,
sacerdotum . . malitia confutanda est 35, 11, gongende 38. 33
(39. 23), ondrædende 98. 16 (99. 19), 124. 35 (125. 24), sleande
158. 26 (159. 24), girmende 166. 25 (167. 18), hergende 168. 34

(169. 24), bærnende 168. 34 (169. 24), donde 230. 18 (231. 7).
No Latin correspondence (50): Hu Sicilia leóde wæron him
betweonum winnende 2. 25, giernende 3. 32, spreccende 6. 7,
wilniende 30. 21, donde 40. 26, 42. 7, dreogende 50, 18, æfterfylgende 50. 23, dreogende 50. 24, forsacende 54. 9, cwiel-
mende 54. 18, donde 54. 22, stellende 64. 24, wenende 76. 15,
farende 76. 20, æfterfylgende 76. 29, wilniende 82. 7, feohtende 82. 12, ondrædende 84. 9, biddende 84. 14, farende
84. 17, winnende 86. 29, wergende 88. 27, winnende 90. 8,
90. 10, hergende, sleande 92. 15, winnende 104. 15, 112. 21,
þrowiende 112. 29, widwinnende 114. 4, hienende 130. 30,
feohtende 132. 24, begongende 156. 1, lærende 162. 27, hergende 172. 34, onwinnende 184. 3, wenende 188. 11, færende
188. 12, þencende 188. 13, æfterfylgende 190. 24, sleande
190. 4, biddende 196. 12, wilniende 202. 10, oþþyncende 232. 21,
biddende 232. 24, farende 246. 8, donde 260. 29, onwinnende
274. 27, wilniende 290. 7.

C. The Periphrastic Present Subjunctive (3).

1. Expresses the Progressive Present (1).
It has *no Latin correspondence* (1): swelce heo selfe
sprecende sie to eallum moncynne 74. 25.
2. Expresses the Indefinite Present (2).
It renders a Latin a) *pres. part.* (1): þær neh sie eft
flowende up of þæm sande 12. 23, profluens 13. 16; b) *infin.*
(1): fol raðe þæs sie east irnende on þæt sond 12. 22, con-
tineo arenis mergi 13. 20.

D. The Periphrastic Past Subjunctive (7).

1. Expresses the Progressive Past (2).
It renders a Latin a) *pres. indic.* (1): swelce heo fleonde
wære 76. 28, simulat diffidentiam 77. 13; b) *infin.* (1): swelce
eal se hefon birnende wære 86. 23, ut coelum ardere visum
sit 87. 10.
2. Expresses the Historical Perfect (5).
It renders a Latin *plup. subj.* (1): witan þæt he .. wið
Alexander fremmende wære 168. 17, quasi urbem regi vendi-

tasset 169. 12. *No Latin correspondence* (4): þel þe hwa
wære ... yfel donde 56. 1, geþafiende 88. 21, wilniende
194. 22, wenende 194, 22.

E. The Copula *weorðan* and the Present Participle.

Expresses the Progressive Past (1).

It has *no Latin correspondence* (1): on þæm fleame
weorð an Ueriatuses þegn þæm oþrum to longe æfterfylgende
216. 21.[1]

PSALMS (15).

A. The Periphrastic Present (7).

I. Accompanied by a temporal modifier expresses the
Progressive Present (1).

It renders a Latin *fut. dep.* (1): ymb his ǽ he byð
smegende dæges and nihtes 1. 2, in lege ejus meditabitur die
et nocte.

II. Without a temporal modifier (6).

1. Expresses the Progressive Present (3).

It paraphrases the Latin (3): beoð ure gear-dagas
gnorn-scendende 89. 10, eardiende 135. 27, lifigende 136. 7.

2. Expresses the Indefinite Present (3).

It renders a Latin a) *perf. indic dep.* (1): unriht he
byð smeagende on his cliofon 35. 3, iniquitatem meditatus
est in cubili suo; b) *perf. pass.* (1): forspyrcende synd mine
mearhcofan 101. 3, ossa mea ... confrixa sunt; c) *paraphrase*
(1): forðon weðearfende þearle syndon 78. 8.

B. The Periphrastic Past (7).

1. Expresses the Progressive Past (2).

It renders a Latin a) *perf. indic.* (1): wæs ic slæpende,
sare gedrefed 56, 4, dormivi conturbatus; b) *perf. indic. dep.*

---

[1] The participle is an predicative adjective in the following
example: wæstmberende 32. 12 (33. 16).

(1): ic ... eam biddende bealde Drihten 141. 1, ad Deum deprecatus sum.

2. Expresses the Historical Past (5).

It renders a Latin a) *perf. indic. dep.* (2): hy wæron wundriende 47. 5, admirati sunt, sprecende 49. 1; b) *perf. indic. pass.* (1): hy ... wæron styriende 47. 5, commoti sunt; c) *fut. pass.* (1): on eallum þinum weorcum ic wæs smeagende 76. 10, exercebor: *No Latin correspondence* (1): he wæs cleopiende to Drihtne 27 rubric.

C. The Periphrastic Imperative (1).

It renders a Latin *fut. pass.* (1): Drihton, for þinum naman beo þu forgifende nimne synna 24. 9, propitiaberis peccato meo.

BENEDICT (9).

A. The Periphrastic Present Indicative expresses the Progressive Present (1).

It *paraphrases the Latin* (1): gif he ... bið ... on modignesse wuniende mid upahefednesse 52. 9 in superbiam elatus 27.

B. The Periphrastic Present Subjunctive (8).

I. Accompanied by a temporal modifier expresses the Imperative (1).

It renders a Latin *pres. subj.* (1): he symble þencende sy on godre drohtunge 115. 23, cogitet 872 D.

II. Without a temporal modifier (7).

1. Expresses the Progressive Present (4).

It renders a Latin a) *pres. part.* + *esse* (4): hwæþer heora anig ... sy God secende 25. 15, si est requirens Deum 372 B, sittende, standende, gangende 31. 7 (374 C).

2. Expresses the Imperative (3).

It renders a Latin a) *pres. part.* (2): ac be fremedum dome and hæse donde sy 20. 12 sed ambulantes alieno judicio

3*

et imperio 350 B, wuniende 49. 17 (507 D), b) *infin.* (1): ne
sy nan lofgeon ne wilnigende 18. 18, non velle dici sanctum
antequam 297 A.[1]

AELFRIC'S HEPTATEUCH (19).

A. The Periphrastic Present (5).

1. Expresses the Progressive Present (3).
It renders a Latin a) *fut. perf.* (1): nu wat heo þæt
heo ys eacniende G. 16. 5 quod conceperit; b) *infin.* (1):
hire innoð ys weaxende G. 38. 24 videtur uterus illius in-
tumescere; c) *pres. part.* (1): cumerde ic eom to eow E. 3. 16,
visitans visitavi vos.
2. Expresses the Future (2).
It renders a Latin *pres. indic.* (2): þe feohtende beoð
wið eow Josh. 10. 25, adversum quos dimicatis, worigende
N. 14. 33.

B. The Periphrastic Past (13).

I. Accompanied by a temporal modifier expresses the
Progressive Past (4).
It renders a Latin a) *perf. indic.* (3): Lange he wæs
feohtende on fyrlenum burgam Josh. 11. 18, multo tempore
pugnavit, wuniende Jud. 3. 30, 8. 28. *Paraphrase* wuniende
G. 16. 1.
II. Without a temporal modifier (9).
1. Expresses the Progressive Past (7).
It renders a Latin a) *perf. indic.* (1): hig wæron þâ
eacnigende G. 19. 36, conceperunt; b) *pres. part.* (3): Israela
folc weox, swilce hig of eorðan spryttende wæron E. 1. 7.
quasi germinantes multiplicata sunt, ondrædende and forbugende Job. 1. 1; c) *infin.* (1): efne wæs þa growende Aarones
gird N. 17. 8 invenit germinasse virgam Aaron. *Paraphrase*
(2): eardigende Jud. 13. 2, Josh. 9. 1.
2. Expresses the Historical Past (2).

---

[1] The participle has an adjectival force in *cariende* 46. 11 (484 D).

It renders a Latin a) *imp. subj.* (1): æle burhwara wæs bugende to him butan Eueum Josh. 11. 19, non fuit civitas quae se traderet filiis Israel praeter Hervæum; b) *perf. indic. dep.* (1): Drihten wæs þa sprecende to Moise D. 32. 48 Locutusque est dominus.

C. The Copula *weordan* and the Present Participle (1).

The Periphrastic Present expresses the Future (1).

It *peraphrases* the Latin: ic worde syddan georwiende G. 42. 38, deducetis canos meos cum dolore ad inferos. [1]

AELFRIC'S COLLOQUIUM (1).

The Periphrastic Present expresses the Progressive Present (1).

It renders a Latin *pres. part.* + *pres. indic. of esse* (1): fordam cild ic eom under gyrda drohtniende 102. 9, quia puer sum sub uirga degens.

AELFRIC'S INTERROGATIONES SIGWULFI (6).

A. The Periphrastic Present (4).

Accompanied by a temporal modifier expresses the Progressive Present (4).

It renders a Latin *adj.* (2): gif heo turniende is humetane feald heo 12. 109, si volubile est, cur non cadat? 13. 8, turniende 13. 108 (13. 7). *No Latin correspondence* (2): wunigende 54. 513, 56. 534.

B. The Periphrastic Past (2).

I. Accompanied by a temporal modifier expresess the Progressive Past (1).

No Latin correspondence (1): se wæs æfre wunigende ær anginne mid him on his bosme 54. 516.

---

[1] In the following examples the participle is a predicative adj.: untymende G. 11. 30, 16. 2, 25, 21, 30. 1, Jud. 13. 2.

II. Without am temporal modifier expresses the Progressive Past (1).

It renders a Latin *pres. part.* (1): þa þa þæt flod wanigende wæs 36. 340, reversæ sunt aquæ de terræ, euntes et recedentes 37. 8.[1]

THE GOSPELS (53).

A. The Periphrastic Present (12).

1. Expresses the Progressive Present (4).

It renders a Latin a) *pres. part.* + *the pres. indic. of esse* (1): Nis nán þing of þam men on hine gangende Mk. 7. 15, nihil est extra hominem introiens in eum; b) *pres. part.* (3): sume synt her standende Mt. 16. 28, sunt quidam de hic stantibus, L. 9. 27, wuniende Mk. 9. 1.

2. Expresses the Future (6).

It renders a Latin a) *pres. part.* + *the fut. of esse* (5): heofones steorran beoð feallande Mk. 13. 25, stellae caeli erunt decidentes, suwiende L. 1. 20, gefonde L. 5. 10, hæbbende L. 19. 17. sittende L. 22. 69; b) *pres. part.* (1): twa beoð æt cwyrne grindende Mt. 24. 41 duae molentes in mola.

3. Expresses the Indefinite Present (2).

It renders a Latin a) *pres. part* + *the pres. indic. of esse* (1): ne synd ge na sprecende ac se halga gast Mk. 13. 11 non enim estis vos loquentes; b) *pres. part.* (1) ne nis yfel treow gódne wæstm donde L. 7. 43 neque arbor mala, faciens fructum bonum.

B. The Periphrastic Past (38).

I. Accompanied by a temporal modifier expresses the Progressive Past (2).

It renders a Latin *pres. part.* + *the imp. indic. of esse* (2): hig wæron symle on þam temple gop hergende > hyne eac bletsigende L. 24. 53, erat semper in templo, laudantes et benedicentes Deum.

---

[1] *Untymende* 46. 441 is a predicative adjective.

II. Without a temporal modifier (36).

1. Expresses the Progressive Past (35).

It renders a Latin a) *pres. part.* + *the imp. indic.* of *esse* (28): ðær wæs soðlice unfeorrann swyna heord ma manegra manna læswiende Mt. 8. 30, erat autem non longe ab illis grex porcorum multorum pascens, licgende Mt. 9. 36, etende, drincynde, wifigende, syllende Mt. 24. 38, lærende Mk. 1. 22, bodigende, adrifende Mk. 1. 39. sittende, þencende Mk. 2. 6. fastende Mk. 2. 18, slapende Mk. 4. 38, hyrmende ceorfende Mk. 5. 5, læsgende Mk. 5. 11, lærende Mk. 14. 49, gebidende L. 1. 10, bicniende L. 1. 22, waciende L. 2, 8. wundriende L. 2. 33, bodigende L. 4. 44, sittende L. 5. 17, waciende L. 6. 22, ut-adrifende L. 11. 14, lærende L. 13. 10, 19. 47, 21. 37; b) *pres. part.* + *the imp. subj.* of *esse* (2): se hælend wæs ana hine gebiddende L. 9. 18 cum solus esset orans, L. 11. 1, c) *pres. part.* + *the perf. indic.* of *esse* (2): Iohannes wæs on westene fulligende > bodiende Mk. 1. 4. fuit Johannes in deserto baptizans et praedicans. d) *pres. part.* (3): he wæs bodiende . . . and hælende Mt. 4. 23, praedicans et sanans, geanbidiende L. 2. 25.

2. Expresses the Future Preterite (1).

It renders a Latin *periphrastic imp. indic.* (1): he to gefyllende wæs on hiersulem L. 9. 31 completurus erat in J.

C. The Periphrastic Present Subjective (1). Expresses the Imperative (1).

It renders a Latin *pres. part.* + *the pres. subj.* of *esse* (1): Sin eower leohtfatu byrnende L. 12. 35, sint . . . lucernae ardentes in manibus vestris.

D. The Imperative (2).

It renders a Latin a) *pres. part* + *the imper.* of *esse* (1): beo ðu onbugende þinum wiþerwinnan hraþe Mt. 5. 25 esto protinus consentiens aduersario tuo; b) *infin.* (1): ne beo ge na hogiende ymb þa morgenlican neode Mt. 6. 34, nolite ergo esse solliciti in crastinum. [1]

---

[1] Unbereude L. 1. 7 is a predicative adjective.

— 40 —

III. IN THE ORIGINAL WORKS.

CHRONICLES (26).

A. The Periphrastic Past (22).

I. Accompanied by a temporal modifier expresses the Progresive Past (8): hie ealle on þone cyning wæron feohtende oþ þæt hie hine ofslægene hæfdon 755 A² (48. 4, 9, 26), wunniende 855 A, onfeohtende 871 A (70. 28), healdende 918 C, feohtende 1066 C (198. 24), tyrwigende 1100 E. (235. 23).

II. Without a temporal modifier (14).

1. Expresses the Progressive Past (8): þy geare Healfdene Norþan hymbra lond ge dælde > ergende (hergende E) wæron > hiera tilgende 876. A, sittende 1052 D (175. 15), 1085 E (215. 33, 216. 24), bringende 1086 E (218. 27), smeagende 1090 E, dreogende 1104 E.

2. Expresses the Historical Perfect (6): Her cuom micel sciphere on West Walas . . > wið Ecgbryht West Saxon cyning winnende wæron 835 A, winnende 867 A, 878 A, feohtende 994 E, wircende 994 E, feohtende 1001 E.

B. The Periphrastic Present Subjunctive (1).

Expresses the Progressive Present (1): beo an scip flotigende swa neh þan lande swa hit nyxt mæge 1031 A.

C. The Periphrastic Past Subjective (2)

I. Accompanied by a temporal modifier expresses the Progressive Past (1): ætywde seo heofon swilce heo for neah ealle þa niht byrnende wære 1098 E.

II. Without a temporal modifier expresses the Progressive Past (1): swilce se beam ongean weardes wið þes steorran ward fyrcliende wære 1106 E.

¹ For convenience I have used A instead of the Anglo-Saxon A employed by Plummer to designate the Parker Ms.

D. The Copula *weorđan* and the Present
Participle expresses the Progressive Present (1): þa wurđe
he efre wuniende mid God Aelmihti on heuenrice 675 E
(36. 33).

LAWS (9).

A. The Periphrastic Present expresses the Progressive Present (1): þær he is sittende on feower healfe his App. XII.

B. The Periphrastic Past expresses the Historical Perfect (5): Ic Ine . . wæs smeagende be þære hælo urra sawla Ine Pref., Edmund I Pref., Edgar Supp. Laws. Pref., sprecende Aelfric Introduction pp. 58. 64.

C. The Periphrastic Present Subjunctive expresses the Progressive Present (2): þæt þu sie þy leng bibbende on eorđan Aelfr. Introd. 4, fastende App. 26. 4.

D. The Periphrastic Present Subjunctive expresses the Historical Past (1): þæt te naenig ealdormanna . . . wære awendende þæs ure domas Ine Pref.

BLICKLING HOMILIES (135).

A. The Periphrastic Present (22).

I. Accompanied by a temporal modifier expresses the Progresive Present (3): mycel leohtfæt . . . biđ á dages and nihtes byrnende 127. 31, færende 19. 20, wesende 19. 26.

II. Without a temporal modifier (19).

1. Expresses the Progressive Present (4): hæl us on eorþan we þe synt on lichomum lifgende 81. 22, blowende 115. 14, rixiende 157. 4, sittende 71. 5.

2. Expresses the Future (10): þys morgenlican dæge ic beo gangende of minum lichoman 139. 19, 141. 34, 143. 2, 147. 23, 29, forgifende 19. 30, geherende 63. 26, miltsiende 19. 30, standende 101. 29, efen þrowiende 19. 30.

3. Expresses the Indefinite Present (5): ða folc þær cumende beoð 209. 18, donde 51. 14, fylgende 23. 11, 243. 33, sittende 23. 8.

B. The Periphrastic Past (111).

I. Accompanied by a temporal modifier expresses the Progressive Past (6): he wæs simle hine to Drihtne gebiddende mid myclum wope 229. 18, donde 223. 30, dwelgende 201. 20, spreccende 223. 30, 231. 32, wæccende 137. 20.

II. Not accompanied by a temporal modifier (105).

Expresses the Progressive Past (22): þa wæs he ealre fægernesse full and he wæs blowende on him sylfum on swyþe manigfealdre wynsumnesse 115. 7, cwepende 151. 10, farende 249. 2, fylgende 155. 26, gongende 141. 23, gripende 211. 1, hleonigende 145. 26, hlifigende 143. 5, hweorfende 67. 10, geseonde 209. 30, singende 147. 3, 149. 23, 151. 9. 231. 9, sittende 67. 36, 155. 27, 28, slæpende 235. 19, stondende 11. 22. wunigende 75. 5, 133. 15, 165. 18.

2. Expresses the Historical Perfect (83): aefter þyssum wordum gefylde, þa wæs Maria arisende 145. 23, blissigende 139. 8, I57. 6, cegende 139. 16, cleopigende 139. 16, cweþende 57. 1, 137. 22, 139. 8, 12, 14, 17, 141, 6, 17, 35, 143. 16, 26, 36. 145. 7, 15, 17, 20, 147. 6, 9, 18, 33, 149. 21, 151. 14, 21, 153. 6, 8, 24, 31, 36, 155. 21, 157. 6, 11, 18, 27, 159. 15, 22, 26, 231. 1, cyssende 157. 27, 237. 24, geféonde 139. 8, 249 16, fylgende 15. 27, 229. 20, 249. 7, gangende 145. 25, 151. 17, 157. 26, ingongende 143. 14, 147. 1, 4, 241. 19, utgangende 145. 23, 149. 22, hweorfende 139. 3, 199. 6, 207. 30, 249. 12, lærende 141. 24, meolcgende 93. 32, secgende 161. 19, geseonde 151. 8, sprecende 5. 2, 39. 24, 55. 2, 61. 28, 153. 33, 159. 25, 235. 27, 32, ðrowiende 237. 10, weþende 141. 35, 151. 20, 249. 7, wundrigende 153. 7, wyrcende 69. 16, 75. 32, wynsumiende 137. 31, 143. 25.

C. The Periphrastic Present Subjunctive expresses the Indefinite Present (1): hie sýn ofergytende þisse sæwe ege 235. 1.

D. The Periphrastic Past Subjunctive expresses the Progresive Past (1): he ateowde us swa he slæpende være to costianne 235. 4.[1]

AELFRIC'S HOMILIES (155)

A. The Periphrastic Present (56).

I. Accompanied by a temporal modifier (17).

1. Expresses the Progressive Present (12): ða wyrta beoð nu to-dæg blowende on wynsumnysse II 464. 13, forbtigende I 408 .30, growende II 406. 20, scinende II 46. 21, wanigende II 214. 33, weallande II 46. 22, weaxande I 154. 27, II 214. 32, 323. 23, wunigende I 282. 14, 324. 19, II 606. 16.

2. Expresses the Future (5): forðan ðe þa mánfullan beoð æfre cwylmigende on helle susle II 608. 11, ðrowigende I 294. 6, wunigende I 160. 17, 276. 17, 606. 2.

II. Not accompanied by a temporal modifier (39).

1. Expresses the Progressive Present (18): se is biddende minre miltsunge mid eornestum mode I 386. 19 (Acts 9. 11), byrnende I 320. 34, 344. 7, 9, godigende I 124. 33. growende I 304. 26, scinende I 118. 6, onsigende II 146. 16, stigende II 76. 18. wanigende I 154. 28, 356. 24, II 76. 21, weaxende I 356. 26, wunigende I 236. 34, 322. 17, 408. 13, 540, 1, wyrcende II 530. 19.

2. Expresses the Future (6): forðon ðe we beoð hæbhende ðæs ðe we ær hopedon I 250. 33, scinende II 322. 11 (Is. 1. 18), sittende I 542. 20, II 248. 19, ðeonde II 74. 13, weornigende I 168. 33.

3. Expresses the Indefinite Present (15): seraphim sind ða gastas gecigede, ðe beoð on Drihtnes lufe byrnende I 348. 26, 540. 13, ofgangende I 280. 14, healdende II 236.

---

[1] In the following examples the participle is a predicative a) adj.: unberende 93. 30, balwende 115. 8, 209. 10, miltsigende 45. 1, 87. 35, 89. 24, 249. 6, scyndende 115. 19, 195. 25, soþsecgende 187. 29, gewitende 65. 15; b) substantive: dælnimende 191. 25, forlærende 141. 2, 149. 13, 16.

18, sittende II 318. 3, forð stæppende I 280. 14, oferstigende
I 262. 11, þeonde II 76. 19, 364. 3, 390. 24, wunigende I
288. 35, II 44. 18, 206. 26, 236 18, wyrcende II 316. 19.

B. Periphrastic Past (84).

I. Accompanied by a temporal modifier express Progressive Past (18): wæron togædre bodigende binnan ðære byrig
seofon monðas þam folce lifes weig I 374. 29, blawende II
350. 9, lærende I 406. 27, tæcende I 442. 29, ðeonde II
334. 2, wunigende I 146. 26, 32, 150, 15, 200. 30, 206. 34,
214. 27, 276. 15, 296. 20, 504. 13, II 4. 23. 42. 8, 64. 13,
198. 12.

II. Not accompanied by a temporal modifier (66).

1. Expresses the Progressive Past (43): hé dyde þæt
hi wæron . . . bodigende ymbe Godes rice I 320. 21, 372.
5, forbugende II 446. 11, byrnende I 320. 20, II 312. 17,
ondrædende II 446. 11 (Job 1. 1), II 446. 30 (Job 1. 8),
drohtnigende I 320. 13, 402. 21, 416. 4, 436. 22, 546. 3,
II 174. 5, fleonde I 372. 17, growende II 144. 11, scinende
II 186. 35, sittende I 572. 12., sprecende I 66. 15, 318. 25,
520. 4, sprengende I 466. 26, steppende II 508. 18, ðeonde
I 614. 17, II 120. 11, 154. 10, 166. 27, waciende I 30. 15
(Luke 2. 8), wanigende I 356. 35, weallende II 350. 7,
wunigende I 20. 6, 106. 9, 136. 3, 148. 3, 150. 3, 222. 17,
232. 27, 23, 308. 20, 314. 4, 404. 30, II 22. 19, 44. 18,
333. 29, 386. 6.

2. Expresses the Future Preterite (1): he . . . bodode
þæt him wæs Godes grama ónsigende, gif hi to Gode bugan
noldon I 246. 17.

3. Expresses the Historical Perfect (22): he wæs ða
biddende his Drihten mid þisum wordum I 382. 21, 426. 1,
bifigende I 504. 28, bodigende I 370. 25, clypigende I 422.
18, cweðende 358. 25, derigende I 414. 16, drohtnigende
II 188. 13, hliddende I 376. 5, scinnende I 62. 30, 540. 27,
544. 32, II 186. 12, 334. 10, sprecende I 608. 4, strynende

I, 308. 22, 26, styrigende I 372. 12, 376. 5, twynigende I 302. 1, ðeonde I 308. 19, forðyrnende I 562. 15.

C. The Periphrastic Present Subjunctive (5).

1. Accompanied by a temporal modifier expresses the Progressive Present (1): þeah ðe hé ungefullod gýt farende sy II 500. 35.

II. Not accompanied by a temporal modifier (4).

1. Expresses the Progressive Present (1): Criste geðafenað þæt he weaxe, and me þæt ic wanigende beo I 356. 27.

2. Expresses the Indefinite Present (3): gif heo hwæt digles on hyre hæbbende sy I, 388. 30, wunigende I 302. 20, II 438. 28.

D. The Periphrastic Past Subjunctive (5).

1. Expresses the Progressive Past (4): gif his hreofla godigende wære I 124. 27, slæpende II 152. 33, wunigende II 252. 33. wyrsigende I 124. 26.

2. Expresses the Historical Perfect (1): þeah ðe he mid eallum mægne wiðerigende wære II 122. 23.

E. The Imperative (4).

Beo heo eac onbyrd and byrnende on Godes lufe swa swa fyr II 46. 5, beon[1] eower leohtfatu byrnende II 564. 25, blowende I 64. 15, wunigende II 252. 21.

I. The Copula weorðan and the Present Participle (1).

The Periphrastic Past expresses the Historical Perfect (1): cweðende I 520. 4.[2]

---

[1] *Béon* is, of course, an infinitive, but is here included on account of its finite use.

[2] In the following examples the participle is a predicative a) adj.: eacnigende I 42. 2, halwende I 122. 10, II 260. 20, behreowsigende

AELFRIC'S LIVES OF SAINTS (83)

A. The Periphrastic Present (13).

I. Accompanied by a temporal modifier expresses the
Progressive Present (5): symble he bið gyfende 1. 46, lifigende
23. 726, smeageude 23. 452, wunigende 16. 1, 218.

II. Not accompanied by a temporal modifier.

1. Expresses the Progressive Present (5): ic me gebidde
to ðam Gode, þe bið eardigende on heofonum 5. 417, gyr-
mende 21. 297, wuniende 1. 19, 177, 13. 196.

2. Expresses the Indefinite Present (3): sume syndan
creopende on eorðan mid eallum lichoman 1. 52, tellende
23 B. 229, tiligende 23 B. 245.

B. The Periphrastic Past (62).

I. Accompanied by a temporal modifier expresses the
Progressive Past (12): oþ þæt þreo and fiftigðe gear he wæs
þær on þam regole drohtnigende 23 B. 47, 803, onsittonde
23. 494, sittende 23, 803, smeagende 31. 28, wexonde 23. 621.
winnende 23 B. 564, 578, 25. 730, wraxligende 23 B. 578,
wunigende 20. 126, 21. 270.

II. Not accompanied by a temporal modifier (50).

1. Expresses the Progressive Past (30): seo wurðfull
byrgen þæs ðe him eallum þuhte eall bifigende wæs 21. 125,
23 B. 232, 461, blætsigende 23 B. 640, creopende 10. 86,
ehtende 23 B. 188, færende 18. 421, 25. 563, wið-feohtende
25. 425, fcohtende 25. 491, 563, fleonde 23 B. 188, gangende
10. 86, behealdende 23 B. 178, herigende 23 B 42, lærende
29. 210, licgende 26. 214, sawende 23 B. 143, sprecende
23. 584, tospræcende 23. 718, for-þyldiende 30. 446, winnende
30. 445, wunigende 3, 566, 6. 131, 13. 148, 202, 16. 162,
21. 447, 25. 277, wyrcende 23 B. 143.

2. Expresses the Historical Perfect (20): þæs þe he
biddende wæs 3. 15, 23 B. 670, brucende 23 B. 35, eft-cyr-

rende 23 B. 641, dælende 30. 9, fægnigende 23. 824, farende
23. 702, hæbbende 23 B. 32, 142, healdende 23 B. 110, rixiende
18. 387, smeagende 23. 222, sprecende 23. 210, 389, 23 B. 51,
standende 23 B. 417, geniht-sumigende 23 B. 395, wundrigende
23. 775, wyrcende 12. 178, 245.

C. The Periphrastic Present Subjunctive
expresses the Indefinite Present (2): eala hwæder heo hider
cumende seo 23 B. 667, wyrcende 23 B. 78.

D. The Periphrastic Past Subjunctive (5).

I. Accompanied by a temporal modifier expresses the
Progressive Past (2): ac wære þæt getél wunigende æfre ne
læs ne má on þæm munuc-life 7. 268, 1. 7.

II. Without a temporal modifier (3).

1. Expresses the Progressive Past (2): þa cunnodan læcas
hwi he licgende wære 7. 67, libbende 23 B. 91.

2. Expresses the Historical Perfect (1): raphahel se
heah-engel wære tó tobíe sprecende 23 B. 7.

E. The Copula *weordan* and the Present
Participle (1).

The Periphrastic Past expresses the Historical Perfect
(1): Zosimus þa sodlice weard micelan gefean cyrrende 23 B.
725.[1]

AELFRIC'S DE VETERE ET NOVO TESTAMENTO (2).

The Periphrastic Past expresses the Progressive Past (2): þe mid þam hælende wæs his agen leor-
ningcniht on þisum life farende 12. 29, wuniende 4. 34.[2]

---

[1] In the following examples the participle is a predicative adjective: halwende 16. 294, styrigende 1. 131, wel-wyllende 3. 417.

[2] Scinende 2. 33 is a predicative adjective.

AELFRIC'S BEDE'S DE TEMPORIBUS (8).

The Periphrastic Present.

I. Accompanied by a temporal modifier expresses the
Progressive Present (4): ðæt æmtige fæc bufon þære lyfte is
æfre scinende of ðæm heofonlicum tunglum 6. 5, weaxende,
waniende 5. 25, yrnende 2. 24.

II. Without a temporal modifier expresses the Progressive Present (4): ác on middan urum wintra beoð hyra
feldas mid weortum blowende 10. 2, waniende 4. 3, weallande
12. 25, weaxende 4. 3.

BASIL'S HEXAMERON (2).

A. The Periphrastic Present expresses the Indefinite Present (1): God geworhte ... eall wyrmcynn ða ðe
creopende beoð 14. 31.

B. The Periphrastic Past Subjunctive ex-
presses the Progressive Past (1): se lifigende God æfre wære
wunigende ærðam ðe he worhte gesceafta 4. 7.

BASIL'S ADMONITIO.

No example.

WULFSTAN'S HOMILIES (33).

A. The Periphrastic Present (11).

1. Expresses the Future (10): ge heofonwered ge eorð-
wered ge hellwered ... bið bifjende 26. 1, 203. 6, byrnende
25. 16, 203. 2, cwacjende 26. 1, 203. 6, ehtende 199. 21,
sweltende 210. 19, 218. 11, lædende 254. 2.

2. Expresses the Indefinite Present (1): he ... byð þeah
smeagende oftor ymbe swicdom, þonne ymbe wisdom 52. 31.

B. The Periphrastic Past (17).

I. Accompanied by a temporal modifier expresses the
Progressive Past (5): þe wæs á nymende earmra manna æhta
on unriht 140. 23, sprecende 222. 34, 235. 17, 27, 237. 4.

II. Not accompanied by a temporal modifier (12).

1. Expresses the Progressive Past (4): he wæs biddende his lifes 237. 8, 259. 10, cwelende 213. 8, eardjende 106. 3.

2. Expresses the Historical Perfect (7): ær wæs eall weoruld sprecende on ân gereord 211. 19, 218. 2, 219. 31, 235. 6, wyrcende 235. 13, wylnigende 11. 7, 278. 12.

C. The Periphrastic Past Subjunctive (4).

I. Accompanied by a temporal modifier expresses the Progressive Past (1): heo wære herigende æfre on hire life ure drihten 237. 14.

II. Without a temporal modifier (3).

1. Expresses the Progressive Past (1): sæde .. þæt heo wære mildheortnesse fyligende 237. 12.

2. Expresses the Historical Past (2): se ðe wære gitsjende oðra manna þinga 72. 3, scaðjende 72. 12.

D. The Copula weorðan and the Present Participle (1).

The Periphrastic Present expresses the Indefinite Present (1): ne ænig man ne gewunje, þæt he mid yfelum wordum to wyrjende weorðe 70. 18.[1]

SALOMAN AND SATURNUS (1).

The Periphrastic Past Subjunctive expresses the Historical Perfect (1): saga me, hwelc man ǽrest wære wið hund sprecende 34.[2]

THE POEMS (19).

A. The Periphrastic Present (3).

1. Expresses the Progressive Present (2): swa þin rice restende bið anwloh for eorlum oþ þæt þu eft cymst Dan.[3] 584 (manet. Dan. 4. 23), ac him bið reordiende Sat. 626.

---

[1] In the the following examples the participle is a predicative a) adj.: mildsjende 229. 13, 26, scinende 8. 2; substantivo: hyrwende, leande, lufjende 82. 1, tiligende 72. 12.

[2] *Berende* 35 is a predicative adjective.

[3] The poems are cited according to the abbreviations used by Grein.

2. Expresses the Future (1): þa ðe firnedon, beoð beofigende, Sat. 621.

B. The Periphastic Past (12).

1. Expresses the Progressive Past (11): swa se halga wer herigende wæs metodes miltse, Az. 49, Dan. 334, beatende An. 1543, weallende An. 1709, ehtende B. 159, secgende B. 3029, gefeonde El. 173, 989, bidende El. 484, drusende,[1] El. 1258, flonde Gen. 2084.

2. Expresses the Historical Past (I): swa ic him sylfum ær secgende wæs, An. 949.

C. The Periphrastic Past Subjunctive (3).

1. Expresses the Progressive Past (2): þæt þu sunu wære efen-eardigende mid þinne engan frean Cri. 236, sincende Gen. 1437.

2. Expresses the Historical Past (1): gif þonne Fresna hwylc .. þæs morðor-hetes myndgiend wære B. 1106.

D. The Imperative (1).

Hal wes þu ... beo þu growende on godes fæþme Charms I. 68.[2]

---

[1] According to Schürmann (p. 319). I should prefer to regard the participle as attributive in this passage.

[2] In the following examples the participle is a predicative adjective; halwend Dóm. 84, unlifgende B. 467, efen-wesende Cri. 349, lifgende Dan. 764, þyrsthycgende Gn. Ex. II 50, tælende Fā. 90.

I. Table giving the Total Number of Periphrases in the Translations with the Latin Forms they Render.

	Bede	Boethius	Gregory	Orosius	Psalms	Benedict	Aelfr. Hept.	Aelfr. Col.	Aelfr. Sig.	Gospels	Total
Pres. Indic.	7	3	4	13	—	—	2	—	—	—	29
Pres. Indic. Pass.	—	—	2	3	—	—	—	—	—	—	5
Pres. Indic. Dep.	1	—	1	—	—	—	—	—	—	—	2
Pros. Subj.	—	1	—	1	—	1	—	—	—	—	3
Pres. Subj. Dep.	—	—	1	—	—	—	—	—	—	—	1
Imp. Indic.	3	—	—	1	—	—	—	—	—	—	4
Imp. Indic. Pass.	1	—	—	2	—	—	—	—	—	—	3
Imp. Indic. Dep.	18	—	—	—	1	—	—	—	—	—	19
Imp. Subj.	4	—	—	4	—	1	—	—	—	—	9
Imp. Subj. Dep.	16	—	—	—	—	—	—	—	—	—	16
Perf. Indic.	2	2	—	28	1	—	4	—	—	—	37
Perf. Indic. Pass.	4	—	—	3	2	—	—	—	—	—	9
Perf. Indic. Dep.	32	—	3	2	3	—	1	—	—	—	41
Perf. Subj.	7	—	—	—	—	—	—	—	—	—	7
Perf. Subj. Dep.	6	—	—	—	—	—	—	—	—	—	6
Plup. Indic.	1	—	—	1	—	—	—	—	—	—	2
Plup. Indic. Dep.	1	—	—	—	—	—	—	—	—	—	1
Plup. Subj.	—	—	—	5	—	—	—	—	—	—	5
Future	—	—	1	—	—	—	—	—	—	—	1
Future Pass.	—	—	—	—	2	—	—	—	—	—	2
Future Dep.	—	—	—	—	1	—	—	—	—	—	1
Future Perf.	—	1	—	—	—	—	1	—	—	—	2
Future Perf. Dep.	1	—	—	—	—	—	—	—	—	—	1
Pres. Indic. Periphr.	1	—	3	—	—	—	—	—	—	—	4
Pres. Subj. Periphr.	2	—	—	—	—	—	—	—	—	—	2
Imp. Indic. Periphr.	1	—	—	—	—	—	—	—	—	1	2
Imp. Subj. Periphr.	10	—	—	—	—	—	—	—	—	—	10
Fut. Perf. Periphr.	—	—	—	1	—	—	—	—	—	—	1
Pres. Part.	125	2	9	20	—	2	4	—	1	8	171
Pres. Part. + esse	—	—	—	—	—	4	—	1	—	43	48
Pres. Part. abl. abs.	7	—	—	1	—	—	—	—	—	—	8
Perf. Part.	29	1	—	4	—	—	—	—	—	—	34
Perf. Part. abl. abs.	1	—	—	4	—	—	—	—	—	—	5
Fut. Part.	6	—	—	—	—	—	—	—	—	—	6
Infinitive	6	—	—	9	—	1	2	—	—	1	19
Supine	1	—	—	—	—	—	—	—	—	—	1
Gerund	—	—	3	2	—	—	—	—	—	—	5
Adjective	2	—	1	—	—	—	—	—	2	—	5
Substantive	—	1	1	26	—	—	—	—	—	—	28
Paraphrase	4	4	1	—	4	1	4	—	—	—	18
No Latin Correspondence	—	5	—	105	1	—	—	—	—	3	114
Total	299	20	30	235	15	9	19	1	6	53	687

4*

II. Table giving the Various Significations of the Periphrasis in the Translations.

		Bede	Boethius	Gregory	Orosius	Psalms	Benedict	Aelfr. Hept.	Aelfr. Col.	Aelfr. Sig.	Gospels	Total
Periphrastic Present	Pres. Prog. .	7	10	1	5	4	1	3	1	4	4	40
	Pres. Indef. . . .	5	3	7	8	3	—	—	—	—	2	28
	Future	2	1	6	—	—	—	3	—	—	6	18
Periphrastic Past	Past Prog. . . .	101	4	2	107	2	—	11	-	2	37	266
	Past Hist.	142	1	5	105	5	—	2	—	—	—	260
	Pluperfect . .	5	—	—	—	—	—	—	—	—	—	5
	Fut. Pret. .	8	—	—	—	—	—	—	—	—	1	9
	Passive	1	—	—	—	—	—	—	—	—	—	1
Periphrastic Present Subjunctive	Pres. Prog.	—	1	3	1	—	4	—	—	—	—	9
	Pres. Indef.	1	—	—	2	—	—	—	—	—	—	3
	Imperative . . .	—	—	4	—	—	4	—	—	—	1	9
	Future . . .	3	—	—	—	—	—	—	—	—	—	3
Periphrastic Past Subjunctive	Past Prog. . .	10	—	1	2	—	—	—	—	—	—	13
	Past Hist.	5	—	1	5	—	—	—	—	—	—	11
	Fut. Pret. . . .	9	—	—	—	—	—	—	—	—	—	9
Periphrastic Imperative . .		—	—	—	—	1	—	—	—	—	2	3
Total .		299	20	30	235	15	9	19	1	6	53	687

III. Table giving the Various Uses of the Periphrasis in the Original Works.

		Chronicles	Laws	Blick. Hom.	Aelfr. Hom.	Aelfr. L. of Sts.	Aelfr. de v. et n. Test.	Aelfr. do Temp.	Basil	Salm. Sat.	Wulfstan	Poems	Total
Pres. Indic.	Progressive	1	1	7	30	10	—	8	—	—	—	2	59
	Indefinite	—	—	5	15	3	—	—	1	—	2	—	26
	Future	—	—	10	11	—	—	—	—	—	10	1	32
Past Indic.	Progressive	16	—	28	61	42	2	—	—	—	9	11	169
	Hist. Perf.	6	5	83	23	21	—	—	—	—	8	1	147
	Fut. Pret.	—	—	—	1	—	—	—	—	—	—	—	1
Pres. Subj.	Progressive	1	2	—	2	—	—	—	—	—	—	—	5
	Indefinite	—	—	1	3	2	—	—	—	—	—	—	6
Past Subj.	Progressive	2	—	1	4	4	—	—	1	—	2	2	16
	Hist. Perf.	—	1	—	1	1	—	—	—	1	2	1	7
Imperative		—	—	—	4	—	—	—	—	—	—	1	5
		26	9	135	155	83	2	8	2	1	32	19	473

II.

USES OF THE PERIPHRASTIC TENSES
IN ANGLO-SAXON.

The aim of the present investigation is to determine the significances of the Anglo-Saxon periphrases formed by means of the present participle and the finite forms of the copulas *wesan, béon, weorðan.*

For the purpose of this study all the monuments of the Anglo-Saxon period that were accessible, have been carefully read and the occurrences noted [1], and in the works which have been translated from the Latin, the passages wherein the periphrases occur have been compared with the corresponding passages of the original. These translations fall into two classes: first, the glosses under which are included the interlinear translations of the Gospels (the Lindisfarne and Rushworth glosses), the Rule of St. Benet, and the Vespasian Psalms and Hymns; secondly, the more formal translations which follow their originals with varying degrees of fidelity, and constitute a large bulk of the Anglo-Saxon prose. These two types of translation have received separate treatment, as has also the more original works of Anglo-Saxon writers.

The Epinal, Erfurt, Corpus, and Leiden glossaries contain no examples of the periphrastic tenses. In a Kentish

---

[1] A list of the texts read will be found on p. 6 ff.

glossary of the IX century (Ms. Cotton Vesp. D VI) *polli-centur* has the half-erased gloss *sint behat* . . . in which we may read behatende, justifying the restoration by Bode 316. 28 (gehatende wæs = pollicetur) and the Lindisfarne gloss to Mt. 14. 7 (gehatend wæs = pollicitus est). In a glossary of the XI century (MS. Cotton, Cleopatra A III) 12 examples occur. The periphrastic tenses render 1 present and 1 future participle, various tenses of deponend verbs 5 times, 1 passive and 1 active verb, and the adjective *effeta (berende bið)* twice. The number of examples is too small to reveal any principle of translation.

The glosses to the Lindisfarne and Rushworth Gospels, however, furnish abundant material. Referring to the statistics (p. 11 ff.) for a detailed account of the various Latin forms rendered by the periphrases, it will suffice here to notice the more salient facts which they reveal. The periphrastic tenses occur 317 times. The perfect deponent is rendered 117 times and has therefore influenced the periphrastic form in nearly 37% of the totel number of occurrences. The reason for this is not far to seek. Throughout these glossaries there is apparent a painful effort to reproduce the Latin constructions as closely as the language will permit, and, frequently, the literalness does great violence to the Anglo-Saxon idiom. [1] The Anglo-Saxon glossator, in rendering a form like *profectus est* Mk. 12. 1, had the choice of glossing it with the simple preterite form *gefoerde*, or, aiming at a closer verbal correspondence, of glossing separately the copula and participle, thus: *færende wæs*. In glossing the participial element of the perfect deponent, he was practically constrained to use the present participle; for the passive force of the past participle made it unsuitable to render the deponent verb, which, although corresponding in form, was widely different in significance. The past participle being thus restricted to the passive voice, the present active participle was substituted as a compromise between

---

[1] „Die sclavische Nachbildung des Lateinischen tritt oft peinlich hervor." B o u t e w e k, p. CVI.

the form and significance of the tense (cf. p. 63), and, with
the copula, is used quite consistently throughout to render
the perfect and other compound tenses of deponent verbs.
The presence of double glosses [1] (as in the case just cited)
exhibiting both the simple and periphrastic past, strongly
confirms this view as they make most manifest the scribe's
hesitation between the meaning of *profectus est* as shown in
the gloss *gefoerde*, and the form which is approximated in
færende wæs. The imperfect indicative also exhibits the
double glosses and to a far greater degree proportionately
than the perfect deponent. 28 examples occur and 19 [2] of
them have the double glosses, as *e. g.* Mt. 13. 1 *he gesætt l
wæs sittende, sedebat*; Mk. 2. 4 *læg l licgende wæs, iacebat*.
Obviously the form of the Latin imperfect can not explain
the use of the Anglo-Saxon periphrasis, since the Anglo-
Saxon simple tense is closer to it in form. Why, then, are
both the simple and periphrastic tenses used? Two ex-
planations present themselves. The first is that there is no
real difference between the two tenses and they are used
indifferently as equivalent forms. But the employment of both
together instead of alternating them and the evident struggle
throughout to render the form as well as the meaning of
the Latin are sufficient reasons for rejecting this explanation.
Assuming, on the other hand, that the periphrasis has
something of the force of the Modern English progressive,
we find that the treatment of the glossator is in harmony
with his renditions elsewhere. The explanation is, in fact,
the same as in the case of the perfect deponents but with
the conditions reversed. In the latter the Latin form has

---

[1] Double glosses to the perfect deponent are found in the following
passages: Mt. 8. 1, 14. 13, 19. 2, 26. 10, 27. 55, 28. 13, Mk. 1. 20, 4. 6,
8. 30, 33, L. 2. 39, 18. 28, J. 1. 20, 18. 20, 20, 21. The Rushworth scribe
has generally chosen but one of the forms offered. The copula has also
occasionally u double gloss, as, *e. g.* Mt. 8. 1 *secutæ sunt = fylgende
weron l sint l gefylgdon* since the glossator seems to hesitate between
the present form of the copula and its preterite force.

[2] Mt. 13. 1, 5. 5, Mk. 1. 6, 2. 4, 15. 3. 11, 4. 37, 5. 42, 10. 32,
14. 35, 54, L. 2. 38, 5. 15, J. 4. 6, 5. 9, 18. 16, 18, 19. 6.

influenced the use of the periphrasis, in the former the Anglo Saxon significance of this tense. The correlation of these two tendencies go very far to explain the double use of the periphrasis in Anglo-Saxon both as a progressive and simple tense. That there should be, in consequence, some weakening of the progressive force is not surprising, but that this force continued in the periphrasis is amply testified by the examples here collected, and its final triumph in the subsequent history of the language.

The 13 examples of the imperfect deponent rendered by the periphrasis fall under the same influences as the other Latin imperfects, but strengthened perhaps by analogy with the compound tenses of the deponent verbs. The perfect passive is rendered 5 times by the periphrasis: *seminatus est* is glossed *sawende wæs* 4 times (Mt. 13. 19, 20, 22, 23) and *contristatus est*, Mt. 14. 9 *unrotsande wæs* once. It is difficult to decide whether the present participle has a passive force in these collocations, or whether we have here errors of translation; the Rushworth glossator in all these passages uses the past participle. Bouterwek (p. civ. f.) has noticed this phenomenon in the following words:

"Eine eigenthümliche Verwendung des part. praes. ist es, wenn das lat. part. perf. dadurch ausgedrückt wird, es also passive Kraft erhält; z. B. seminatus Mt. 13. 19 ff.: sawende, benedicti 14. 61: đæs gebloendsendes . . . Sehr wahrscheinlich beruhen diese Ungewöhnlichkeiten mehr auf Verschlechterung der Mundart und sind Zeichen später Zeit, als dass sie einem tieferen Sprachgesetze folgen".

The Latin periphrastic tenses formed with the future participle and the copula, are rendered 32 times. As the Anglo-Saxon speech has but one active participle it is forced to do yeoman service in rendering the Latin present participle, the perfect participle of deponent verbs, the future participle, and, in a few rare instances, to take on even a passive force. The rendition of the periphrases formed with the Latin present participle and the copula by the same Anglo-Saxon periphrases calls for no comment. They are so rendered 54 times. The present participle used attributively is rendered 12 times, the absolute participle 5 times, the perfect participle 6 times and the future participle 5 times. Other Latin forms so rendered are given in the statistics. In the Rule of St. Benet 9 examples occur. 3 of these are interesting as showing a still further extension of the present participle as a gerundive, and equivalent to the inflected infinitive. Ex.: þara wacmodes from þam abbote is to forsceawiende 84. 6 quorum imbecillites ab abbate consideranda est. So: 5. 14, 26. 11. (Cf. Logeman § 89).

The 95 occurrences in the Vespasian Psalter and Hymns contain 75 renditions of the perfect deponent. Here we have not the helpful double glosses, but, confirmatory of the slavish literalness exhibited in the other glosses, the copula is rendered 32 times in these examples by the present instead of the past tense. The perfect passive is rendered twice and the remaining examples divided between other tenses of deponent verbs and the present participle.

The glosses from their very nature reveal to a marked degree the influencee of the Latin originals, but the scribe's treatment of the perfect deponent and the imperfect tenses, affords us data upon which it can be confidently asserted that the progresive force of the periphrases was already a possession of the language, however obscured by the tendencies we have just considered.

In the translations from the Latin, there are 687 examples of the periphrases distributed as follows: Bede 299, Boethius 20, Gregory 30, Orosius 235, Psalms 15, Benedict 9, Aelfric's Heptateuch 19, Aelfric's Colloquium 1, Aelfric's Interrogationes Sigewulfi 6, Gospels 53. The copula weorðan is employed 3 times to form the periphrasis; the copulas béon and wesan together 684 times. The periphrases are thus divided among the moods and tenses: Present Indicative 86, Past Indicative 541, Present Subjunctive 24, Past Subjunctive 33, Imperative 3.

The Present Tense expresses progressive action 40, indefinite action 28, and the future 18 times. In the examples expressing progressive action, the verb is accompanied 20 times by temporal modifiers enforcing the idea of continuance.

Exs : se nu gyt lifigiende is, Bede 4. 12; for þæm hit is nan
tweo þæt þa godan bioþ simle wealdende, Boeth. 178. 5;
hwæt is ðonne ðæt rice and se ealdordom butan ðæs modes
storm se symble bið cnyssende ðæt scip, Greg. 58. 5; se
ðe ana is god þæt he is wunigende . . . æfre on þrim hadum
butan onginne > ende Aelfr. Sig. 54. 513. Many of the
verbs like *lifigende, eardiende, wunigende, ricsiende, wealdende,* etc. are from their nature continuous. 2 examples are
influenced by the Latin periphrasis of the present participle
and *esse*: Aelfr. Col. 102. 9, Mk. 7. 25.

The Indefinite or Aoristic Present is found 28 times.
It renders the present 6, the perfect 2, the present participle
8, an adjective 1, a perfect participle 1, the present participle + esse 1, and the gerund 2 times. In 1 example it
paraphrases the Latin and in 5 there are no Latin corres-
pondences. Exs.: swylce hit is berende on wecga orum, aser
> isernes, leades > seolfes, Bede 26. 14; an ðara gecynda
is þæt heo biþ wilnigende oþer þ heo biþ irsiende Boet. 132.
4. Seo . . . is irnende þurh middewearde Babylonia burg,
Oros. 74. 3.

The 18 examples expressing the Future have usually
a future participle in the original, and 5 occurrences in the
Gospels are due to the present participle and the future of
esse in the Vulgate. Exs.: se þe demende is cwicum > deadum. Greg. 96. 13, qui judicaturus est vivos et mortuos 66.
19. Likewise 441. 20. be þære we nu sindon sprecende
Bede 172. 25, de qua sumus dicturi, 288. 16. þu byst onweald hæbbende ofer tyn ceastra L. 19. 17. eris potestatem
habens super decem civitates.

The Periphrastic Past Indicative occurs 541 times. It
is quite evenly divided between the progressive and historical
tenses, as there are 266 examples of the first and 260 of the
second. It expresses the pluperfect 5 times, the future preterite
9 times, and the passive once.

The Progressive Past is accompanied in 119 examples
by various adverbial modifiers denoting continuance. The most
numerous class of adverbial modifiers is the accusative of
extent in time, which is found 53 times: 16 times in Bede,

35 times in Orosius, and twice in the Heptatench. These 53 examples of the progressive force of the tense are among the clearest we have. Exs.: seo mægþ ðreo gear fulle in gedwolan wæs lifigende, Bede 142. 14. he ða se arwyrða Godes ðeow monig gear in Mægilros ðæm mynstre drohtniende wæs, Bede 364. 15. hi ða X gearþa burg sittende wæron > feohtende, Oros. 50. 13, hie Scipia wæs ealle þa niht sleande ... oþ dæg Oros. 200. 20. Two examples of the adverbial genitive are found in Bede: he wæs mycelre tide on Hybernia Scotta ealonde wunigende 168. 29. So: 272. 18. Temporal adverbial phrases accompany the periphrasis 12 times in Orosius. These time-phrases are *on symble, on þære hwile, on þone tide, mid þam þe, on ðæm dagum*, etc. Exs.: on þære ilcan tide wæron ... wifman winnende in Asiam 170. 13; mid þæm þe he sprecende wæs to his geferum, 84. 33, hio ðyrstende wæs on symbel mannes blodes, 30. 27. Temporal adverbs strengthen the progressive force of the tense in 30 examples, distributed as follows: Bede 13, Orosius 12, Heptateuch 2, Interrogationes Sigewulfi 1, Gospels 2. Of most frequent occurrence is *symble*; others are *dæghwamlice, á, gelomlice, gena, longsumlice unablinnendlice, longe, oftrædlice*, etc. Exs.: seo rihtgelyfde láar wæs dæghwamlice weaxende, Bede 246. 32; mid þa he þa gena wæs begeondan sæ wuniende Bede 458. 7; ægþer ge þe men ge ða nytenu unaablinnendlice piniende wæron, Oros. 36. 31, þa wæron simbel binnan Romebyrig wuniende, Oros. 72. 1, hi wæron symbel on þæm temple god hergende > hyne eac bletsigende L. 24. 53. There are 20 examples of the periphrastic past accompanied by the conjunctive adverb *oþ*. Mätzner (II. 32) says of this form: "The endeavor also often appears to give to the action a certain perpetuity: Hî ealle þa þone cyning wæron feohtende oð þæt hý hine ofslagene häfdon (Sax. Chr. 755)". Here the adverb by setting a limit to the duration of the action seems to emphasize its continuance up to that limit. The action is represented (1) as advancing to a definite end; as, Perseus ... on ða ðeode winnende wæs oþ hi him gehyrsume wæron, Oros. 40. 32; or (2) the action is continuous for a time until another event brings it to a close; as, he on anre stowe ... wæs wuniende

oþ he his lif forlet, Oros. 220. 2. In both cases the duration
of the action is dwelt upon. Exs.: (1), him Ciras wæs æfterfylgende oþ he hiene gefeng > slog Oros. 74. 33. Hi . . . on
ðæt folc winnende wæron > þa wepnedmen sleande oþ hie
ðæs londes hæfdon miccl on hiora anwalde Oros. 46. 5; (2)
wæs þæt folc þonan ut sleande > hienende oþ þæt Hanra . . .
hiene æt þam fastene gesohte mit XXM. Oros. 168. 29. One
example of the periphrasis with an accusative of extent in
space occurs in the account of Wulfstan's voyage: Wulfstan
sæde þæt he gefore of Hædum, þæt he wære on Truso on
syfan dagum > nihtum, þæt þæt scip wæs calne weg yrnende
under segle, Oros. 19. 34. Here the idea of duration is
derived from the length of the voyage, and enforced, perhaps,
by the temporal phrase preceeding, on syfan dagum > nihtum.
In one rare example a temporal prefix is attached to the
verb: he wæs sinþystende monnes blodes, Oros. 130. 34.

There are 147 examples of the progressive past not
accompanied by temporal modifiers, and they render various
Latin constructions. The present participle is so rendered
48 times, 34 of which occur in Bede. The periphrasis in these
examples are often found in temporal clauses, and are due
to the expansion of an apposative participle or participial
phrase into a clause. Exs.: þa he arisende wæs Bede 378. 22,
resurgens autem sensit. mid þy he þa wæs eft hweorfende
to Breotone, Bede 462. 1, qui cum Britaniam remeans. gelomp
sume dæge ða we ferende wæron mid hiene, Bede 398. 29.
contigit die quadam nos iter agentes cum illo. Many of these
clauses would be rendered in modern English by the apposative participle, and it is curious that the Anglo-Saxon trans-
lator, who in very many instances is all too servile an imi-
tator of the Latin, should depart from his original when so
much would have been gained by adhering to it.

The periphrasis formed by the Latin present participle
and the copula, has, in the Gospels, influenced the construction
43 times. In 30 examples the participle is found with the
imperfect indicative. Exs.: swa hi wæron on þæm dagum
ær þam flode, etende, and drincende, and wifigende, and gyfta
sellende, oð þone dæg þe Noe on þa earce eode Mt. 24. 38,

sicut erant in diebus ante diluvium, comedentes et bibentes, nubentes et nuptum tradentes, usque ad eum diem quo entravit in arcam noe. þær wæron sume of ðæm bocerum sittende > on heora heortum þencende Mk. 2. 6, erant autem illic quidam de Scribis sedentes et cogitantes in cordibus suis. He wæs on scipe ofer bolster slapende Mk. 4. 38 erat . . dormiens. he wæs dæghwamlice on þam temple lærende L. 19. 47 erat docens quotidie in templo.

In many instances our only guide is the context, as the Anglo-Saxon often gives a very free paraphrase of the Latin, or, as is especially true of the Orosius, additions are made for which we seek vainly in the sources. But some verbs are from their nature continuous, as, e. g. *wunian, eardian, lifigean*, and those expressing growth and decrescence like *weaxan, wanian, growan*. Exs.: wæron þær monige byscope sittende mid Johannes þone apestolican papan, Bede 460. 27. wæs sum munuc > mæssepreost in nehnesse his ectan eardigende Bede 434. 9, him þa siþþan se freondscipe wæs betweonum weaxende Oros. 232. 27. siþþon wæs farende þær ðæs cyninge modor mid þæm twæm dælum þæs folces wuniende wæs. Oros. 76. 21. ân man wæs eardigende on Israhêla þêode Manne gehaten Iudges 13. 2. Similarly in Num. 17. 8, Josh. 9. 1. A state of mind may in some instances be described by the progressive form. Exs.: Dameris mid micelre gnornunge ymb þæs cyninges slege hiere suna þencende wæs, hu heo hit gewrecan mehte, Oros. 76. 24. Theodosius wæs þencende hu he Gratianus his hlaford gewrecan mehte, Oros. 292. 23.

The periphrastic past is an historical tense almost as often as a progressive tense, and its restriction to the latter use must be sought for in a subsequent period of the language. Which use is original and which developed can not be determined with certainty. The treatment of the Latin imperfect in the Lindisfarne gloss seems to favor the view that the progressive force was original, and that the employment of the periphrasis in historical tenses developed through the effort of translators to render the Latin depo-

nent verbs and periphrastic tenses. Certainly there can be
no question but that these latter forms have greatly influenced the extension of the use of the periphrasis in
Anglo-Saxon, and they have, probably, weakened its primary
significance. In Bede 32 examples are traced to these
forms. Schmidt (p. 55) says:

"Einen weiteren Beweis, wie eng sich König Aelfred
an die Wortformen der Vorlage hielt, liefert die Art und
Weise, wie er lateinische Deponentia übersetzt. Dass die-
selben activische Bedeutung hatten, sah er wohl; aber die
passivische Form veranlasste ihn doch, wenigstens äusserlich
dadurch eine Aenlichkeit mit dem Lateinischen zu erreichen,
dass er deponentiale Bildungen durch Zusammensetzungen
von Participien Praes. mit bêon ersetzte, ähnlich wie ja Ver-
bindungen der Participia Præter. mit beon zur Vertretung des
Passivums dienten."

Exs.: he wæs ðæm broðrum cidende > ðus cwæð. Bede
366. 4, protestatus est fratribus, dicens. hraþe ða gefremednesse ðære arfestan bene wæs fylgende, Bede 32, 8, et mox
effectum piae postulationis consecutus est. ða æfter ðon ðe
se here wæs ham hweorfende Bede 54. 7, at ubi hostibus
exercitus . . domum reversus est. God wæs biddende, Bede
154. 21, Dominum deprecatus est. sylce eac on ða tid . . .
wæs ðrowiende Scs. Albanus Bede 34. 8, si quidem in ea passus
est sanctus Albanus. Weran þrowiende þa forsprecenan Cristes
þeowas . . . þy fiftan dage Nonarum Octobrium, Bede 416. 29,
passi sunt autem praefati sacerdotus.

Schmidt (p. 55) says further:

"Im Orosius ist die Zahl solcher Bildungen wie *feohtende
wǣron* = pugnabant eine ungemein grosse, und man könnte
es daher auch im Beda für eine rein zufällige Erscheinung
halten, dass gerade Deponentia oft durch derartige Wendungen
übersetzt sind, zumal da eine konsequente Durchführung nicht
zu bemerken ist, allein es ist hier deutlich zu verfolgen, dass
in den meisten Fällen, in denen ein Part. Praes. mit dem
Verbum substantivum verbunden ist, im lateinischen Original
ein Deponens vorliegt".

While this statement is essentially correct, exception must be taken to the observation that this method of translating the other tenses of deponent verbs is a purely accidental phenomenon. It is due, rather, to direct analogy of the perfect deponent under which influence the periphrasis is, by a natural extension, employed to render the other tenses of deponent verbs.

In the translations, the periphrastic tense is traced to a present participle in the original 171 times, to a perfect participle 34 times, and to the future participle 6 times. The perfect indicative chiefly with verbs of motion, influences the construction 37 times. The frequent employment of the periphrasis with these verbs has already been noticed by Hickes. Very many examples, especially in Orosius, show no Latin influence whatever. Many verbs in these examples describe military operations; as, *æfterfyligian, winnan, hergian, feohtan, bærnan, slean.*

A striking illustration of the desire to render the Latin present participle by the periphrasis is furnished by a passage in the Heptateuch where, under the influence of the present participle, tense sequence is completely violated: Cumende ic eom tô éow and ic geseah ealle þa þing þe éow gelumpon on Egiptalande, Ex. 3. 16, visitans visitavi vos et vidi omnia quae acciderunt vobis in Agypto. The Vulgate here uses the participle adverbially according to the Hebrew idiom [1] in which the infinitive absolute is so used to give an intensive force to the verb. (Cf. Gensenius's Hebrew Grammar § 131. 3 a).

The Periphrastic Past has the force of the perfect 5 times in Bede. The verb *spræcan* is used 4 times in this way: bi ðam we foresprecende wæron 66. 1 de quibus præfati sumus. So: 202. 25, 276. 28, 324. 11; and *forlætan* once: 262. 32.

The periphrasis has in one passage the force of the passive, but this should probably be regarded as a scribal error since the other MS. uses the past participle: neh ceastre

---

[1] פקו פקרתי

gehwylee > land wæs forhergiende (MS. B. reads *forheregeodc wæron*), Bede 52. 29 proximas quasque civitates agrosque depopulans 74. 4.

The periphrasis expresses the future preterito 9 times of which 8 examples occur in Bede. In each case the Latin has a future participle. Exs.: ða bæd he his þegn on æfenne þære neahte þe he of worulde gougendc wæs Bede 346. 29, noete qua de seculo erat exiturus. þætte þæt seolfc leoht þa sawle þara Cristes þeowa wæs gelædende > onfonde Bede 284. 22, quae animas famularuin Cristi esset ductura vel susceptura in coelio. So: 108. 11, 458. 15, 16. One example is curious on account of the sequence of tense: ðis syndon ðan fyr ða ðe middangeard wæron forbærnende > forneomende Bede 212. 25. If we read *aron* for *wæron* it would have the force of the simple future.

The periphrastic present subjunctive expresses the present progressive 9 times, the present indefinite 3 times, the imperative 9 times, and the future 3 times. Examples of the progressive present: hio wind wid ða gōd ðe mon ær gedon hæfð, buton mon simle swincende & wyrcende sie god weorc oð ende Greg. 445. 15. heo wære to bisene asteald eallum middangearde > eac swelce heo self sprecende sie to eallum moncynne Oros. 74. 25. swa swa hwær he sy sittende, standende oð þe gangende onhuigenum hæfde his gesyhðe aduna on eorðan besette, Benedict 31. 7. In three examples the periphrasis has the force of the simple (indefinite) tense: sume men secgan þæt [Nilus] . . . þonne folroðe þæs sie east irnende on þæt sond > þonne besinc eft on þæt sand, > þær neh sie eft flowende up of þæm sande, Oros. 12. 20 – 23. So also Bede 480. 11. The imperative force is shown in the following examples: ac sic se lareow eallum monnum se nihsta & eallum monnum efndrowiende on hiera geswincum Greg. 96. 22 ; so: 60. 13. 124. 4, 5. he symle þencende sy and hine swylcne on godre drohtunge hine gegearwige, Benedict 115. 23; so: 18. 18, 20. 12, 49. 17. Examples of the future: seo wise hwelcne ende hæbbende sie, sio æfterre eldo gesið > sceawað, Bede 480. 12, quae res quem sit habitura finem; so: 476. 30. þæt we men monede ðy læs we ænige tide ussum licumlicuin

unalefednessum sion þeowiende Bede 356. 12. In the last
example futurity is weak and follows from the idea of possibility.

The periphrastic past subjunctive is found 13 times as
a progressive tense, 11 times as a historical tense, and
9 times as a future tense. The progressive tense is accompanied 3 times by temporal adverbs: *gena, gyt, symble.* Exs.:
sæde eac se ylca broþur ða gyt on ðam mynstre lifigiende
wære. Bede 188. 1; so also: 378. 12, 188. 6. It expresses
the progress of a disease: seo sona wære to ðon swiðe
weaxende > hefigende þæt se earm wæs ... gecerred, Bede
392. 4; recurrent action: awritan is þæt hi wæron todælende
heora weoruld god, Bede 66. 2. Other examples are Bede
66, 2, Boet. 46. 25. It expresses the future preterite 9 times.
The Latin periphrastic subjunctive has influenced the tense
5 times. Exs.: cwæð he þætte sawl butan ængum sare ...
wæs utgangende of lichoman, Bede 269. 11, dixit quod anima
ejus et sine dolore ... esset egressura de corpore * 52. 23;
so: 102. 25, 286. 25, 288. 20, 368. 20. In the other examples
the future is derived from the idea of possibility expressed
by the verb. The historical perfect occurs 5 times in Bede,
3 examples being due to present participles in the Latin; as,
is þæt sæd þæt he . . wære arisende of his settle of middan
his ealdormannum > his witum, Bede 470. 61, ut exsurgens
de medio optimatum suorum concessu genua flecteret * 284.
9; so: 306. 23, 368. 16. The present indicative is once
rendered: he gesætte þæt se þe lifigende wære ðæs hades
hæfde mihte, Bede 146. 21, is, qui superest, censors ejusdem
gradus habeat 246. 35. In Gregory the single example is
due to a Latin perfect deponent: hit is awritan ðæt Dina
wæs utgongende sceawian ðæs londes wif, 415. 14. egressa
est Dina 336. 12. In Orosius there are 5 occurrences. In
4, the Latin is loosely paraphrased: Hannibal .. sæde, ðeh
ðe he wilniende wære > wenende Romana anwealdes, þæt
hit God ne geþafode 194. 22; so: 56. 1, 88. 21. Once the
pluperfect subjunctive is rendered: þa tugon hie hiene þære
burge witan þæt he heora swicdomes wið Alexander fremmende wære, > hine for þære tihtlan ofslagon 168. 17, hunc

mortuo Alexandro Carthaginem reversum, quasi urbem regi venditasset, necaverunt, 169. 11.

The present participle is found with the imperative of béon 3 times, once in the Psalms and twice in the Gospels. Exs.: ne beo ge na hogieude ymb þa morgenlican noode, Mk. 6. 24. beo ðu onbugende þinum wiþerwinnan hraþe Mt. 5. 25. Drihten, for þinum namon, beo þu forgifende minne synna Ps. 24. 9.

The copula *weorðan* is used in the periphrasis but 3 times. It expresses the future twice: ðinra synna ne weorðe ic gemunende, ac gemun ðu hiora, Greg. 413. 23; so also: Gen. 42. 38. It expresses the progressive past once; on þæm fleame weorð an Ueriatuses þegn þæm oþrum to lange æfterfylgende, oþ mon his hors under him ofsceat, Oros. 116. 20.

The periphrastic tenses occur 454 times in the more independent prose, and 19 times in the poems. These occurrences are thus distributed: present indicative 117, past indicative 317, present subjunctive 11, past subjunctive 23, imperative 5. The employment of the periphrases in progressive and historical tenses in these works shows only a slight variation from their uses in the translations, but there is, on the whole, a small relative increase of the progressive force. In the present indicative the periphrasis is employed 59 times as a progressive tense and 26 times as an indefinite tense, while in the translations the ratio is 40 to 28. In the past indicative, the increase of progressive use is less marked. The ratio of this to the historical is 169 to 147, and in the translations 266 to 260, an increased use of 3 per cent. This percentage of increase would be somewhat augmented if we excluded the thirteenth of the Blickling Homilies (Assumptio S. Mariae Virginis) which, in some eleven pages, contains more examples of the periphrases than all the rest of the homilies in this collection together. In this homily the periphrasis rarely shows the progressive force. In the present subjunctive tense the progressive force shows some decrease, but the total number of examples is very few. In the past subjunctive, there is a slight increase of the

progressive use. In the Chronicles and in all the works of
Aelfric the progressive use largely preponderates over the
historical use of the periphrasis, in Wulfstan the two uses
are very nearly balanced, while in the Laws and the Blickling Homilies the historical use of the periphrasis is largely
in excess of the progressive.

The periphrastic present indicative represents the progressive present 59 times, the indefinite present 26, the
future 32, and the imperative once. The progressive present
is accompanied 24 times by temporal modifiers denoting continuance. These are á (3), æfre (9) symble (3), hwiltidum (2), nu
(2), nugyt (1), nu to dæg (1), healfum monde (1), dæghwamlice (2).
Exs.: þa wisnode he on Cristes haligra heortum and is nu
on urum heortum blowende Bl. Hom. 115. 14; Aelmihtigan
Godes Sunu is æfre of dæm Fæder acenned and æfre mid
him wunigende Aelfr. Hom. II 606. 16; dæghwamlice dæs
mona byd weaxende odde waniende feower pricam þurh
þære sunna loman, Aelfr. de Temp. 5. 25; rihtwisra sidfæst
is swilce scinende leoht, and weaxende symble od sodre
fulfremendnysse, Aelfr. Hom. II 322. 23. Once the copula
weordan is found: þa wurde he æfre wuniende mid God
Aelmihti on heuenrice, Chron. 675 (p. 36). In 25 examples
no temporal modifier is present. The periphrasis is formed
with verbs of rest; as, wunian eardigan, sittan, libban, and
verbs denoting physical change; as, growan, weaxan wanigen,
which are by nature progressive: with verbs of motion; as,
feohtan, herigan, winnan, faran, gangan, fylgian, and verbs
of saying and thinking; as bodigan, cwepan, sprecan, which,
according to the context, may be progressive or indefinite.
Exs.: þus feor sceal beon þæs cinges grid fram his burhgeate,
þær he is sittende, Laws, App. XII, ubi residens erit; þu
oferswiþdest deaþ, and þu eart rixiende on þinum wuldre,
Bl. Hom. 157. 4; hi sind byrnende na on fyres wisan, ac
mid micelre lufe þæs Wealdenden Cyninges, Aelfr. Hom. I.
344. 9, syddan hi growende beod, he geswycd þære wæte-
runge, Aelfr. Hom. I 304. 26; witodlice seo dwyre sawul
is on sibbe wunigende on hire dæge, Aelfr. Hom. I 408. 13.

The indefinite present occurs 27 times with various verbs. Exs : gif ge me gehyrnď and ge me beoď fylgende, ne án loc of eowrum heafde forwyrď, Bl. Hom. 243. 33; ealle ure corþan wæstmas beoþ gebetsode gif we beoþ riht donde, Bl. Hom 51. 14; se ďe is . . . calle gesccafta healdende butan gesewinc Aelfr. Hom. II. 236. 18; ge beoď mine frynd, gif ge wyrcende beoď ďineg ďe ic bebeode Aelfr. Hom. II 316. 19.

The Future is expressed 32 times by the periphrastic present, and in 5 examples is accompanied by the adverbs æfre and á. Exs.: ďa synfullan beoď on hellewite á ďrowigende, Aelfr. Hom. I 294. 6; þa mánfullan beoď æfre cwylmigende on helle susle, Aelfr. Hom. III 608. 11; þys morgelican dæge ic beo gangende of minum lichoma, Bl. Hom. 139. 19; Forþon on domes dæg beoþ from Gode þysne cwide geherende, Bl. Hom. 63. 26; ealle middaneard biď þonne on dæg byrnende, Wulfst. 25. 16; þa ďe firnedon, beoď beofigende, Sat. 621. As béon is used indiscriminately for the present and future, it is not allways possible to determine which tense it is intended to express.

The periphrastic past indicative expresses the progressive 169 times, the historical 146 times and the future preterite once. The progressive past is accompanied 48 times by various adverbial modifiers denoting duration. These are: (1) The oblique cases of substantives: the genitive and instrumental once each, the dative 3 times, the accusative 9 times Exs.: heo wæs wæccende dæges and nihtes and hic gebiddende æfter Drihtnes upstige Bl. Hom. 137. 20; wæs eallum þam fyrste wunigende binnan þam Godes temple, Aelfr. Hom. I 146. 26; se Hælend wæs wunigende binnan ďæm temple of ďisum dæge oď nu on ďunres dæg. Aelfr. Hom I 214. 27; þy ilcan geare ferde to Rome mid micelre weorpnesse > þær wæs xii menaþ wuniende Chron. 855; wæron togædere bodigende binnan ďære byrig seofon mouďas þam folce lifes weig, Aelfr. Hom. I 374. 29; ďy cahtoþan geare þæs ďe heo Myrcna anweald mid riht hlaford dome healdende wæs Chron. 918 C. (2) Adverbial phrases (3): hi . . . swiďe heardlice lange on dæg feohtende wæron,

Chron. 1066. seo wæs .. on oðre sidan ... blawende
butan forlætnysse, Aelfr. Hom. II 350. 9. So: Chron. 871
A. (3) Temporal adverbs: æfre (14), þa gyt (6), á (3), dæghwamlice (3), lange (3), simle (1). Exs.: hine ða acende
mid soðre mennisenysse, se ðe æfre wæs wunigende on god-
cundnysse mid his Fæder, Aelfr. Hom. I 200. 30; þe wæs
á nymende earma manna æhta on unriht Wulfst. 140. 23;
he wæs simle hine to Drihtne gebiddende mid myclum
wope Bl. Hom. 229. 18. (4) The Chronicle has 3 examples
where the periphrasis is accompanied by the conjunctive adverb oþ: hie þa ymb þa gatu feohtende wæron oþþæt hie
þær inne fulgon, 755. The two other examples are also
found in the entry for this year. In 121 examples the
periphrasis has no temporal modifiers. About 50 distinct
verbs are found, some of which, are by their nature continuous denoting natural changes or a state of rest; as, *blowan
growan, weaxan, wanian, licgean, sittan, slæpan, drohtnigan,
wunigan*. Verbs of motion and verbs of saying and thinking
also occur in the progressive tenses. Exs.: he wæs blowende
on him sylfum on swyþe manigfealdre wynsumnesse Bl. Hom.
115. 7; Iohannes soðlice wæs wanigende on his hlisan Aelfr.
Hom. I 356. 35. ða Willelm Englalondes cyng þe þa wæs
sittende on Normandige ... þis ge axode he ferde into
Englalande, Chron. 1085; þa wæs þær an mæden licgende on
paralisyn lange gebrocod, Aelfr. L. S. 26. 214; ac hwæt
mænde þæt syxtig wera strongera þe þær stondende wæron
ymbe þa reste Bl. Hom. 11. 22. on Decius dæge ... wæs
se halga biscop Sextus on Romana byrig drohtnigende, Aelfr.
Hom. I 416. 4. Eala reowlic > wependlic tid wæs þæs
geares þe swa manig un gelimp wæs forð bringende Chron.
1086 (p. 218); se cyng wæs smeagende hu he mihte wrecon
his broðer Rodbeard swiðost swencean, Chron. 1090; þa
ascán leoht ofer hieora heaford, mid þi se halga Andreas
þanon wæs farende, Bl. Hom. 249. 2. hie wæron eft ham
hweorfende, þonne eodan hie him togeanes Bl. Hom. 67. 10;
Isaias se witega wæs awæg færende, Aelfr. L. S. 18. 421;
he to þære byrig com þær se bisceop on wæs lærende Aelfr.
L. S. 29. 20; an æþele læce wæs wunigende on þære byrig

Aelfr. L. S. 3. 566. man feredc anre wuduwan suna lîc
ðær Petrus bodigende wæs Aelfr. Hom. I 372. 5; se wer
wæs ondrædendo God and forbugende, yfel Aelfr. Hom. II
446. 11 erat vir illc simplex et rectus, ac timens Deum et
recedens a malo, Job 1. 1; ða wæron hyrdes on þæm earde
waciende ofer heora eowede, Aelfr. Hom. 30. 15 (Luke 2. 8);
an þara âwrât Mattheus, þe mid þam hælende wæs his agen
leorning cniht on þisum life færende, Aelfr. de v. et n. Test.
12. 29 swa se halga wer herigende wæs metodes miltse, Az.
49, rodera wealdend þreo niht siddan in byrgenne bidende
wæs, El. 484.

The periphrasis expresses the historical perfect 146
times. 83 examples are found in the Blickling Homilies of
which 60 occur in the thirteenth homily (Assumptio S. Mariae
Virginis). This homily is remarkable for the extraordinary
frequency with which this periphrasis is employed. In some
11 pages it occurs 80 times while all the other homilies in
the collection taken together show only 75 examples. Flamme
must have had this homily in mind when he referred (§ 81)
to "die ausserdentlich häufige Umschreibung des Aktivs durch
das Participium Praesens mit einer Form von *beon, wesan*" in
the Blickling Homilies. The other homilies, as we have seen,
do not exhibit an unusual number, but the thirteenth shows
probably a larger proportionate use of the periphrasis than
any other piece of Anglo-Saxon prose. Hickes remarked the
frequent use of the periphrasis in the Pseudo-Gospel of
Nicodemus (see p. 2) but an extract from this work, "The
Harrowing of Hell", published in Prof. Bright's Anglo-Saxon
Reader, pp. 129—141, though nearly of the same length as
the homily, contains but 41 examples. In the Chronicles the
historical perfect is expressed 6 times. The verbs are *feohtan* (2)
winnan (3) *wyrcan* (1). Exs.: her com se here to Exan mudan >
up eodan to ðere byrig > þær fæstlice feohtende wæron, Chron.
1001; hie late on geare to þam gecirdon þæt hie wiþ þone here
winnende wærun Chron. 867. The Laws contain 5 examples:
smeagan (3) *sprecan* (2). Ic Ine wæs smeagende be þære hælo
ûrra sawla, Ine, Preface; þis sindon þa domas þe se Aelmihtiga
God self spæcende wæs to Moyse, Aelfred, Intro. 49. The

Blickling Homilies in 83 examples contain but 22 verbs
but some of them recur a number of times: *cweþan* 35,
gongan (including *in-* and *ut-gongan*) 9, *hweorfan* 4, *sprecan* 8, *fylgean, wepan, wyrcean* each 3 times. Exs.: þa com
se eadiga Johannes and wæs ingongende of þære halgan
Marian huse Bl. Hom. 143. 14; se eadiga Andreas þe wæs
eft hwyrfende on Marmodonia ceastre Bl. Hom. 249. 12;
forgif me Drihten, þæt ic to ðe sprecende wæs swa to men
Bl. Hom. 235. 32; læt þis þus wesan, god weorc heo wæs
wyrcende in me Bl. Hom. 69. 16; halette on hie mycelre
stefne, and wæs cweþende Bl. Hom. 143. 16; þa ahof
Petrus his stefne and wæs cweþende Bl. Hom. 145. 17.
Aelfric's Homilies contain 23 examples, chiefly with verbs
of saying: *biddan, bodian, clypian, cwedan, sprecan.* Exs.:
se eadiga martyr ða wæs biddende his Drihten, Aelfr.
Hom. I 426. 1; wæs Petrus bodigende geleafan ðæm leod-
scipum, Aelfr. Hom. I 370. 25; se Wealdend Hælend þus
be him cwedende wæs, Aelfr. Hom I 358. 25; ure Drihten
wæs spræcende þisum wordum to his leorning-cnihtum, Aelfr.
Hom. I 608. 4; næs ic ðe derigende on ænigum ðingum,
Aelfr. Hom. I 414. 16. Aelfric's Lives of Saints contains
21 examples with various verbs. Exs.: he wæs eft-cyrrende
þurh þone ylcan sidfæst þes westene þe hé ær þyder becom,
Aelfr. L. S. 23 B. 641; monega cynegas wæron myslice geworhte æfter þysum rixiende in israhela rice, Aelfr. L. S.
18. 189. þa þa hi þæt gewrit ræddon, hi ealle wundrigende
wæron, Aelfr. L. S. 23. 775; Zosimus þa soðlice weard micelan
gefean cyrrende, Aelfr. L. S. 23 B. 725. Wulfstan's Homilies
contain but 8 examples: *sprecan* occurs 4 times, *wyrcean*
once, *wylnian* 3 times. Exs.: ær wæs ealweoruld sprecende
on an gehriode, Wulfst. 219. 31; þa wæs he wilnigende to
gode sylfum geornlice and manigfealdlice, Wulfst. 278. 12.
The poetry furnishes a single example: swa ic him sylfum
ær secgende wæs, An. 949

In Aelfric's Homilies the periphrasis expresses the future
preterite once: he ferde and bodode þæt him wæs Godes
gramma ónsigende, gif hi to Gode bugan noldon I 246. 17.

The Periphrastic Present Subjunctive occurs 11 times.

In 5 examples it expresses the progressive present and is twice accompanied by temporal modifiers. Exs.: Martinus me bewæfde efne mid dyssere wæde, þeah ðe he ungefullod gýt, farende sy, Aelfr. Hom. II 500. 35; þæt þu sie þy lcng libbende on eorðan, Laws, Aelfr. Introd. 4; Criste gedafenað þæt he weaxe, and me þæt ic wanigende beo, Aelfr. Hom. I. 356. 17. In 6 examples it expresses the indefinite present. Exs.: sprec to þinum discipulum . . . þæt sy geblissod heora heorte and hie sýn ofergeotende þisse sæwe ege, Bl. Hom. 235. 1; eala hwæðer heo hider cumende seo, and me ne gyme, Aelfr. L. S. 23 B. 78.

The Periphrastic Past Subjunktive is progressive in 16 examples, of which 5 are accompanied by the temporal adverbs æfre and gyt, and one is accompanied by the accusative of extent in time. Exs.: Toforan sẽe Michaeles mæssan ætywde seo heofon swilc heo for neah calle þa niht byrnende wære, Chron. 1098. ac wære þæt getél wunigende æfre ne læs ne má on þam munuc-lífe, Aelfr. L. S. 6. 268; se lifigende God æfre wære wunigende ar ðæm ðe he worhte gesceafta Basil 4. 7. So: Aelfr. L. S. 1. 7; Wulfst. 137. 14. Ða fandode fordweard scipes hwæder sincende sæflod þa gyt were under wolcum Gen. 1437. There are 10 examples without temporal modifiers. Exs.: sumne æfen wæs gesawen swilce se beam ongeanweardes wid þes steoran ward fyrcliende wære, Chron. 1106. he atewde us swa he slæpende wære to costianne, Bl. Hom. 235. 4. So: Aelfr. Hom. ll 152. 33. he demde þæt he sceolde beon ascyred from manna neawiste gif his hreofla wyrsigende wære odðe betwux mannum wunian gif his hreofla godigende wære Aelfr. Hom. 124. 27. þæt þu sunu wære efen-eardigende mid þinne engan frean Cri. 236. The periphrastic past subjunctive expresses the historical perfect 7 times. Exs.: þæt te nænig ealdormanna . . . wære awendende þas ure domas, Ine Pref.; þeah ðe he mid callum mægne widerigende wære, Aelfr. Hom. II 122. 23.

The Periphrastic Imperative occurs 5 times. Exs.: beoð blowende and welige hwilwendlice þæt ge ecelice wædlion, Aelfr. Hom. I 64. 15; beon eower lendena ymb-gyrde, and eower leohtfatu byrnende, Aelfr. Hom. II 564.

25; hal wes þu . . . beo þu growende on godes fæþme, Charms I 68.[1]

With respect to the origin of the periphrasis, the evidence of the statistics is not conclusive. If the periphrasis is not native, the freedom and frequency of its use shows that it was early naturalized and thoroughly. The influence of Latin appears chiefly in extending its use, as it is frequently employed to render the different periphrastic tenses of Latin, and those tenses of deponent verbs to which the periphrasis bears some resemblance in form, but it is by no means restricted to these tenses. It is, moreover, found freely used in those portions of the literature that are least under Latin influence, and with a better regard for its progressive force. The fact that the periphrasis is used with great laxity, does not indicate any uncertainty as to its force, nor does it indicate that it is a foreign idiom. The language was slowly developing literary form, and precedents had not yet fixed a limit to the uses of the periphrasis.

---

[1] The present participle occurs predicatively with a purely adjectival function a number of times both in the translations and in the more original works, and expresses a state or quality. The occurrences are cited in notes at the end of the statistics of the separate works. A few participial nouns are also cited in these notes.

III.

THE PERIPHRASTIC TENSES IN OTHER LANGUAGES.

The periphrasis which we have been considering is not a special characteristic of any language or group of languages, but is found in all periods of the Indo-European speech, as well as in the Semitic tongues. In Hebrew and Syriac it is used regularly to express the imperfect (cf. Gesenius's Hebrew Grammar § 134. 2c) and the influence of Hebrew has probably extended its use in later Greek. In Sanskrit "combinations of participles with auxiliary verbs of condition or motion, forming phrases which have an office analogous to that of verb-tenses, are not unknown in any period of the language" (Whitney § 1074).

In classical Greek, the construction is found (according to Kühner II § 353) chiefly in poetry, though the prose writers, especially Herodotus, also employ it. It is frequent in Attic prose when an action is represented as continuing. Alexander finds that the participles which lend themselves easiest to this periphrasis, are such as have become adjectivized, while few are found which retain completely their participial force. In these latter cases "the combination was felt to do some violence to the language, and becomes more harsh as the meaning of the participle lends itself less easily to being conceived as a quality" (Alexander, Am. J. Ph. IV. 304).

According to Winer (p. 437 f.) the conditons are much
the same in New Testament Greek: "The present participle
is frequently found (in 'the historical style) in combinations
with the verb *εἶναι*, especially with *ἦν* or *ἦσαν*, though also
with the future. Sometimes this combination appears to be a
simple substitute for the corresponding person of the finite
verb... More frequently, however, it is used to express that
which is lasting (rather a state than an action) — a meaning
which can also be expressed though less distinctly in relation
to what is past, by the form of the imperfect tense: Mk. xv. 43
ἦν προςδεχόμενος τὴν βασιλείαν τοῖ Θεοῦ (L. xxiii. 5), A. viii. 8,
etc. ... This use of the partic. is by no means foreign to
Greek writers... In late writers and in the LXX this construction is much more common though in the case of the
LXX it was seldom suggested by the Hebrew. In Aramaic
however, as is well known, the use of the partic. and verb
substantive as a periphrasis for the finite verb had become
established, and thus, in Palestinian writers, there may have
existed a national preference for this mode of expression."
Green (p. 328) is more direct and speaks emphatically for
the progressive force in the LXX. He says: "A compound
(or resolved) Imperfect (impf. of *εἰμί* and pres. part. of verb)
throws emphasis on the continuity of the action".

In classical Latin, Draeger (Syntax der Lateinischen
Sprache I 293 f.) finds the periphrasis rarely employed except
by Plautus and Terence who use it often. He cites the following exs.: Cic. de or. 3. 12 ær cedens est. Bell. Hisp. 29
currens erat. Ovid her. 18. 55 nox erat incipiens. Sen. ep.
85. 16 si beata vita nullius est indigens. Dræger continues:
"Es scheint hierin zwar ein Graecismus vorzuliegen, indess
mag es eher eine allgemeine Spracherscheinung sein, auch im
Altdeutschen vorkommend, wie Nibelung. 17 mit klage ir helfende vil manec frowe was, 9 daz wil ich immer mere mit
triwen dienende sîn." In late Latin, however, the periphrasis
is found often enough, especially in the Vulgate. "Die Vulgata bildet in den aus dem Griechischen übersetzten Büchern
gleich dem Englischen, mit dem Part. Praes. und dem Verbum
subst. eine periphrastische Conjugation zur Umschreibung des

Verbums finitum, z. B. Eccli. 51. 9 Et vita mea appropinquans erat in inferno. 10 Respiciens eram ad adiutorium hominum. Mark 1. 4 fuit Johannes in deserto baptizans." Cf. also Milroy p. 18 f. Hartel (Wölfflin's Archiv. III. 1 f.) has examnied the Latin of Lucifer of Cagliari and finds in no other text such frequent employment of the periphrasis. He says that there is no active form of the indicative or conjunctive which is not rendered by the present participle and the corresponding form of *sum* (p. 36). With respect to the value of the periphrasis in Lucifer, he says (p. 39): Diese Vorliebe für Zusammensetzungen aber würde man schlecht verstehen, wenn man sie auf eine Verfeinerung des Ausdruckes zurückführte und Unterschiede der Bedeutung zwischen ihnen und den einfachen Formen herausklügelte. Solche sind schlechterdings nicht vorhanden; selbst die an sich richtige Beobachtung, dass die Partizipien bestimmter Verba wie negens, credens, cupiens am häufigsten auftreten, führt zu nichts. Die Vorliebe für Neubildungen im sprachlichen Leben lässt stets mit grosser Wahrscheinlichkeit vermuten, dass die alten das Gepräge, das ihren Kurs gab, verloren haben oder zu verlieren beginnen. Eine Sprache auf diesem Grade der Entwickelung wie die lateinische vermag nicht das alte Gepräge neu aufzufrischen, sie greift, was die romanischen Sprachen lehren, zu Umschreibungen, die durch Umfang kompensieren, was ihnen an innerem Gehalt abgeht."

In the Romance languages the periphrases were formed with *esse, stare, ire, venire,* and the present participle. The first is found abundantly. "Esse hat die Bedeutung eines beharrlichen Seins angenommen; das damit begleitete Part. drückt daher eine beharrliche Thätigkeit aus. Diese nun veraltete Redeform war ehedem sehr gebräuchlich" (Diez p. 908). Diez has collected a number of examples of the periphrases in the Romance languages from which the following are selected: It.: perdante (for perdanti) sono; son di molte pene sofferante; chi è di mi ferente. Span.: merezientes erades; yo desto so creyente; eran creyentes que. Prov.: cum lo leos es dormens; quant la vida er durans; O. Fr.: vos pri que ne seiez fuiant; sont disanz; n'est hurgemont durant. According

to List (Französ. Stud. I 10 f.) the periphrasis with *estre* and
the present participle became obsolete earlier than the periphrasis with *aller*. Examples of both periphrases are frequent
in the XV century, and Marot (1497—1544) still uses both
constructions often, though Montaigne (1533—1592) uses only
the periphrasis with *aller*. The periphrasis with *estre* continues, nevertheless, for some time longer and List gives two
examples from a writer as late as Voiture (1598—1648).
Turning to the Germanic group, we find in Gothic
abundant examples of the periphrasis. According to Bernhardt (p. 320): In abstracter Bedeutung bildet visar die Verbindung zwischen Subjekt und Prädikat . . . Das Prädikat
ist ein Part. Präs., um die Dauer eines Zustandes zu be-
zeichnen, nicht selten für ein einfaches griech. Verbum,
z. B. I Kor. XI. 2 gamunandans sijuþ *μέμνησθε* . . . Am
häufigsten erscheint das Prät. vas in solcher Verbindung."
Douse (p. 244) recognizes the progressive meaning of the
tense, but gives no examples of the present tense. He says:
"A continuative past tense (fashioned on the Greek) is formed
by *was*, *wesum*, etc., and the active ptcp.; as: Was Jōhannēs
daupjands (Mk. 1. 4) = 'John was baptizing'; Wesum sipōn-
jōs fastandans (III. 18) = 'The disciples were fasting', or
'used to fast.'" Grimm (IV. 5), while citing parallel constructions from the Greek, seems still to regard it as merely
equivalent to the simple tense: "Schon Ulf. lässt diese Umschreibung spüren: vas laisjands Matth. 7. 29 scheint gleichviel mit laisida; ist usfalljondō II Cor. 9. 12 gleichviel mit
usfulleith; doch in beiden Stellen gewährt auch der gr. Text
ἦν διδάσκων, ἐστι προσαναπληροῦσα: allein II Cor. 13. 11
εἰρηνεύετε gegeben, gawairthi taujands sijuth! = taujith! Luc.
2. 33 ja vas Jósêf jah aithai is sildaleikjandōna geht wiederum
der Urtext schon voraus *καὶ ἦν Ἰωσὴφ καὶ ἡ μήτηρ αὐτοῦ
θαυμάζοντες",* etc. (Cf. also Gering in Zschr. f. d. Phil. 5. 423 f.)
Passing on to its use in Old High German, Grimm finds it
frequently used to render deponents and the related Latin
periphrasis. "Ungleich öfter", he says, "begegnet die Aus-
drucksweise im Ahd. und zumal beliebt ist sie bei O.: pirum
zelenti (molimur) Dieut. 1. 493; wârin zilênti (molirentur)

1. 520; niozanti wârun 1. 499; der Glossator will fast damit
das lat. deponens erreichen. Der Übersetzer des Is. drückt
locutus est aus durch ist sprechhenti und was sprehhenti;
mensus est durch was mezssendi. K 22 a steht erkebanter
ist für redditurus est. 20 b sî furimakanti (sit praevalens) . .
Allzu häufiger Gebrauch der Umschreibung hebt aber ihre
Bedeutsamkeit auf und bei O. drückt sie in der That meisten-
teils nur das reine Tempus aus. Im T. finde ich sie nur da,
wo die Vulgata darauf führte: warun wahhantê inti bihatentê
(erant vigilentes et custodientes) 6. 1; was sin fater inti muoter
wunterontê (erant pater et mater ejus mirantes) 7. 7". Erd-
man finds the progressive or durative force in both the Old
and Middle High German. In treating of the periphrastic
present (§ 139) he says: "Zur Hervorhebung der dauernden
Handlung diente im Ahd. und Mhd. die Verbindung von *sein*
mit dem Part. Präs.: Otfried. I. 4. 34 *ist er fon jugundi filu
fastênti.* — Mhd. Greishaber Predigten (Stuttgart 1844) 1. 84
der sin dedarf unde ouh bedurfende ist Iw. 4172 *als ich des
beitende bin.* — Nhd. kaum noch üblich: *ic bin das nicht vermutend.* Further on (§ 146) he considers the preterite form
of the periphrasis: "Einen dauernden Zustand in der Ver-
gangenheit bezeichnet *ich war* mit dem Part. Präs.,'; vgl. *ic
bin* beim Präsens § 139. Diese Umschreibung kommt Ahd. und
Mhd. öfters vor, z. B. O. I. 4. 5. *wârun sie reht minnônti.* 10 sô
wârun sie unz an enti thaz lib leitenti (jedoch ohne Bedeutung
einer Dauer I. 4. 57, 58 u. a.). Nib. 1007 *mit klage ir helfende
dâr manec frouwe was.* 2249 *ja was nû niemen lebende al
der degene.* Jetzt wenig mehr üblich; etwa: *ich war mir's
nicht vermutend.*" Cf. also Diez p. 908. Its employment, in
Middle High German, to express continuous action is especially emphasized by Paul § 288: "Statt des einfachen Präs.
oder Prät. eines Verbums kann die Umschreibung durch
das Präs. oder Prät. des Verbums *sîn* mit dem Part. Präs.
angewendet werden, aber immer nur, wenn die Handlung als
eine dauernde gedacht wird; die Umschreibung mit dem Prät.
hat demnach die Bedeutung des lateinischen Imperfektums." Cf.
further Grimm IV. 5 and Vernalaken p. 18 f. In New High
German the participle occasionally retains its verbal function,

but it is generally adjectivized. Cf. Vernalaken p. 17 who cites several examples from Goethe (ich bin sehr erwartend, ich werde jetzt erst recht verlangend) in which the verbal force of the participle remains. Grimm (IV. 6) notes a few examples in Old Norse and Old Danish but says it is much rarer in the North Germanic group.

It appears from the foregoing rapid survey that the periphrases are used in other languages, some of which are widely separated from each other, to express continuance either of an act or of a state. This force, however, gives way partially to the simple tense force under various conditions. The periphrasis loses its progressive force in Lucifer through its substitution for tenses that are obsolete or obsolescent. In German the progressive force continues, but beside it the simple tense value also, especially where it is employed to render Latin deponents and other tenses with which it may have a formal resemblance, conditions which we have seen. obtain equally in Anglo-Saxon. In the Romance languages it appears to have generally preserved the progressive force but succumbed before the rise of other forms. In Anglo-Saxon it is found both as a historical and progressive tense. The development of compound tenses in English no doubt released the periphrasis from its employment in the former capacity, and led to its restriction to the progressive use for which it is so admirably adopted.

IV.

RESULTS.

The periphrasis formed with the present participle and the copula *béon, wesan, weordan*, has in Anglo-Saxon a great variety of uses. In the glosses, it is chiefly employed to render the perfect indicative of deponent verbs, the Latin periphrastic tenses, and the imperfect. The perfect indicative of deponent verbs is rendered oftener by this periphrasis than any other Latin tense, and this construction is evidently so employed on account of its outward resemblance to the Latin tense. The absence of a future active participle in Anglo-Saxon has caused this periphrasis to be also used to render the Latin periphrasis in which this participle is employed; when so used the Anglo-Saxon periphrasis has frequently a future force. The Latin periphrasis formed with the present participle and *esse* is, as we should expect, rendered by the parallel Anglo-Saxon construction, with which it is identical both in form and meaning. In the Rule of St Benet the periphrasis renders the Latin periphrastic passive tenses in a few instances.

In the translations, the periphrasis is freely employed and has a number of different functions. In the present tense it expresses the indefinite and progressive present, the future and the imperative; when employed as a progressive tense it is frequently accompanied by determinations of time, enforcing the progressive idea. The past tense is found very much oftener than the present tense, and is, for the most part, used to express the progressive and historical past. The progressive past is frequently accompanied by adverbial modifiers expressing continuance and these emphasize the progressive force of the verb. The historical past is found often with verbs of motion, but other verbs are not wanting, especially verbs of saying and thinking. This periphrasis also expresses the future preterite (the Latin usually has a future participle), to a less extent the pluperfect, and once the passive. As in other languages the participle often becomes a simple adjective, and less often a substantive.

In the more original works, the periphrasis is chiefly restricted to the progressive and indefinite or historical tenses, but in the present tense, the future also appears frequently. As in the translations, the progressive tenses are here also often accompanied by temporal modifiers. The imperative is here found in its own mood, and not in the subjunctive, as is usually the case in the translations. The future preterite occurs once. The participles figure here also occasionally as adjectives and substantives. The progressive use is relatively larger than in the translations, but the increased use is slight.

The influence of the Latin has tended to greatly increase the employment of the periphrasis, but it has, at the same time, greatly obscured the progressive force.

BIOGRAPHICAL SKETCH.

I was born in New York City on Sept. 9, 1864. I entered the University of Texas, Austin, Tex., when it was opened in the fall of 1883, and received the degree of B. Lit. in 1886. In September, 1891, I reentered the University of Texas and studied English Literature and Philology under Prof. Waggener and Dr. Callaway, and Teutonic Philology under Dr. Primer. In 1892 I received the degree of A. M. In the fall of the same year I entered the Johns Hopkins University and chose English as a major subject, and German and French as minor subjects. Here I have studied under Prof. Bright and Prof. Browne, Prof. Wood and Dr. Learned, Prof. Elliott and Dr. Matzke, and Prof. Bloomfield. To my instructors at both institutions, I wish to express my deep appreciation of their many kindnesses. I wish also to thank Mr. Uhler of the Peabody Institute and his associates in the Library for the many courtesies shown me while pursuing the present investigation.

www.ingramcontent.com/pod-product-compliance
Lightning Source LLC
Chambersburg PA
CBHW020311090426
42735CB00009B/1313